AUSTIN

MURDER&MAYHEM

RICHARD ZELADE

THE
History
PRESS

Published by The History Press
Charleston, SC
www.historypress.net

Copyright © 2015 by Richard Zelade
All rights reserved

First published 2015

Manufactured in the United States

ISBN 978.1.62619.917.0

Library of Congress Control Number: 2015948350

CONTENTS

Introduction 5

How Do You Say "Please Don't Kill Me" in Comanche? 7
"Shoot, Damn You, Shoot!" 9
Texas "Swing" 13
"Hold Fast What You Get and Catch What You Can" 17
Assassination in the Most Public of Places 21
"Killed in the Line of Duty" 27
"Are You as Good a Man as You Was a While Ago?" 35
Big Ben 39
"My Amen Is Happiness to Come" 63
The Servant Girl Annihilators 79
"Should We Have Another Such Legislature, Would It Not Be Well
    to Dissolve Our State Government and Get Attached
    to the Indian Territory?" 95
"Why Don't You Use It, Now That You Have Your Hand on It?" 105
Love Lies Bleeding in Their Arms 111
Legal Lunacy 115
"Tell Ben I've Killed Mollie" 125
Adamant Johnson 137

Bibliography 141
About the Author 143

INTRODUCTION

Austin is the spawn of murder and mayhem.

If you are a Bible-toting Texan like most of us are, murder and mayhem go back to Cain and Abel and have been faithfully practiced ever since, Austin being no different than any locality of any size anywhere. This compendium of crime runs from the founding of Austin through the end of the Roaring Twenties. Not that murder and mayhem haven't continued to thrive in our pretty little city, but you can only stuff so many tawdry tales into one slim volume.

Most of the stories I have chosen, I realized as I was wrapping up the manuscript, involve the three Ls: lawmakers, lawmen and lawyers, with some soldiers and servant girls thrown in. Was this the product of serendipity? Or some sort of Freudian flippancy? After all, I have always enjoyed taking pot shots at the pillars of our society, à la John Dowell. I can't decide myself.

HOW DO YOU SAY
"PLEASE DON'T KILL ME" IN COMANCHE?

In his welcoming address to Republic of Texas president Mirabeau Lamar on October 30, 1839, Edwin Waller, chief contractor and Austin's first mayor, noted that since his construction crew had commenced building Austin in May of that same year, they "were liable every moment to be interrupted by the hostile Indians, for whom we were obliged to be constantly on the watch; many-tongued rumor was busy with tales of Indian depredations, which seemed to increase in geometrical progression to her progress through the country."

The March 11, 1840 issue of the *Austin Sentinel* featured a remedy against Indian arrows, given by Henry Mollhausen, captain of artillery and Austin's first architect: "Take 16 to 24 sheets of blotting paper, interspersed with layers of silk or cotton, wrap it around your torso like a jacket, and you will be invulnerable to arrows and bullets." The *Sentinel* also printed a brief dictionary of the Comanche language for the convenience of its readers.

The city was thrown into considerable excitement two nights later, when a man named Ward, a butcher, was found dead. His corpse was shockingly mangled—shot with three rifle balls and an arrow and scalped by a party of Indians who had ventured into town for the purpose of plundering and stealing. Scouting parties immediately got up and made an unsuccessful search. The next morning, another corpse was found about a mile below town—that of a ditcher, Thomas Hedley. He was attacked while alone, in his camp. Endeavoring to escape, he had gotten some two hundred yards from the camp, in the direction of the city. He was pierced with twelve arrows (most of which passed through his body), his throat was cut from ear to ear and he had been scalped. Future Texas president Anson Jones noted in his diary that the suburbs of the town had been plundered of all the horses and he heard Hedley's cries while under the hands of the Indians.

The good citizens of Austin were so rattled that Mayor Waller felt compelled to issue a public declaration on March 15, urging everyone to preserve strict quiet, "avoiding all unnecessary noise of any description, particularly the discharge of fire arms." Acknowledging a likely repeat of the events of the thirteenth, he laid out a plan of action:

> *It is expected that every citizen will have his arms in order for immediate use. Any incursion of hostile Indians into the City will be denoted by two discharges of the Cannon, which is under the direction of Captain Henry Mollhausen, and the Citizens are requested upon hearing the report, to assemble instanter, at the office of the Quarter Master General, on Congress Avenue opposite the Capitol, where those who require it, will be furnished with arms and ammunition. Particular attention is requested to these suggestions, that unanimity and vigor of action may be insured and the apprehension of the female portion of the community, in some degree quieted.*

That night, Secretary of State James Mayfield was slightly wounded by a shot fired by an Indian while escorting a lady from a party to her home.

The Indians were skulking about through the streets at night with impunity during the summer of 1841, frequently dressed in white men's clothing. Scarcely a night passed without someone seeing Indians in town; they were thick as hops, and occasionally they knocked over a poor fellow and took his hair.

During November, the Indians were daily robbing and murdering the inhabitants on the frontiers, frequently in sight and in hearing of this city. When Congress came into session, the cannon was stationed in the street with the expectation of an attack from the Indians.

But there was danger lurking within, as well as without.

"SHOOT, DAMN YOU, SHOOT!"

In a state where some of the highest elected officials make no secret of the fact that they carry concealed weapons on their person at all times, it should not be surprising that politics in Texas has long been—and still is—a deadly game.

As recently as the 2015 legislative session, a representative from Houston cursed a colleague on the House floor before threatening to hurt a Department of Public Safety officer, according to the officer's incident report.

Political violence in Texas precedes the founding of Austin.

James Collinsworth, Peter Grayson and Mirabeau Lamar were locked in a bitter, three-way race for the presidency of Texas in 1838. On May 24, Grayson accepted a candidacy for the presidency. Shortly afterward, he was chosen to serve as minister plenipotentiary to the United States. On his way to Washington, he shot himself to death on July 9 in Tennessee. Since Sam Houston could not succeed himself as president, James Collinsworth was chosen as the Houstonian party's nominee. On July 11, Collinsworth died after jumping off a boat in Galveston Bay after a week of drunkenness. Lamar won the election.

Austin became the most enduring fruit of Lamar's victory.

In 1842, the capitol building was a cabin of rough Bastrop pine with two large rooms, one each for the House and Senate.

After the House of Representatives had adjourned for the evening on January 6, 1842, David Kaufman, the former Speaker of the House of Representatives, who had represented Nacogdoches County from 1838 to 1841, attacked former secretary of state Mayfield, now the member from

AN EX-CONGRESSMAN CANING GRAVES FOR SLANDER!—See chap. xv.

From The Great Iron Wheel Examined; or Its False Spokes Extracted, and An Exhibition of Elder Graves, Its Builder, *William G. Brownlow, 1856.*

Nacogdoches, because of some very pointed and severe remarks Mayfield had made in the House earlier that morning about Kaufman's political character.

Immediately after adjournment, Kaufman walked up to Mayfield in the passage between the Senate chamber and the House, raised a stick in a threatening position and commenced drawing a pistol. Mayfield, who had been previously cautioned and furnished with weapons, drew a pistol. Kaufman could not get his pistol out, so he retreated, passing off the end of the gallery, and made a show of continuing the fight. Mayfield fired two pistols in succession, the second of which took effect on Kaufman, entering the upper part of the abdomen.

Kaufman suffered very much, and it was feared that the wound was mortal, but he recovered. After Texas became a state, he represented the

Eastern District of Texas in the United States House of Representatives during the Twenty-ninth, Thirtieth and Thirty-first Congresses.

Mayfield was freed on $5,000 bail and was acquitted in district court.

Like many of his contemporaries, Mayfield had a volatile character. On the evening of March 15, 1846, Mayfield, Bartlett Sims of Bastrop and Judge Robert M. "Three-legged Willie" Williamson were together in a room at Swisher's hotel, engaged in conversation, when Mayfield took offense at something Sims said. Mayfield promptly drew a pistol and was about to shoot him. Sims was a powerful man, and Williamson was rather below the medium size and slim. In order to avoid being shot, Sims grabbed Williamson in his arms and held him between himself and Mayfield, exclaiming: "Shoot, damn you, shoot!" Williamson did not like his position between Sims and Mayfield, who was trying to get a shot at Sims without harming the judge. Williamson was unable to help himself, so he vented his feelings in alternate expressions of eloquent imprecation and denunciation.

Williamson first earnestly appealed to the belligerents, saying, "Gentlemen, this matter can be settled amicably; there is no necessity for bloodshed. For God's sake, Mayfield, don't shoot!" Then, as Mayfield pointed the pistol at Sims, Williamson said, "Mayfield, make a center shot; for, damn you, I will kill you, sure, if my life is spared!"

"Bart, damn your soul, let me down!" From this appeal, or threat, or for some other reason, Mayfield cooled down and desisted. Mayfield afterward swore that Three-legged Willie saved Sims's life on the occasion.

Mayfield was born in Tennessee in 1809 and moved to Texas in 1837. In January 1839, he was practicing law in Nacogdoches. Mayfield represented Nacogdoches County in the Fifth and Sixth Congresses and served as Lamar's secretary of state for several months in 1841.

In September 1842, Mayfield assembled a company of volunteers from La Grange to help repel the Mexican army then occupying San Antonio. His group and several others arrived at the scene of the Mexicans' massacre of Nicholas Dawson's company on Salado Creek while it was occurring. Mayfield decided that his group was too far outnumbered, so they stood back until the next day, when they joined Mathew Caldwell's company in time to help bury their fellow countrymen. He presented himself as a candidate for major general of the Texas army in 1843 but then withdrew, claiming ill health. Or did Caldwell's and Edward Burleson's accusations of his cowardice at the Dawson massacre provoke his decision? Mayfield represented Fayette County at the Convention of 1845 regarding statehood and, during the same year, challenged Burleson to a duel before backing out.

In April 1846, Mayfield helped organize the Democratic Party in Texas. He was living in La Grange in 1849, the year he killed Absolom Bostwick in a political argument. "General" James Mayfield, described as "an eminent lawyer of La Grange," died in December 1852 in Gonzales.

Bartlett Sims was born in Tennessee about 1792 and settled in present-day Wharton County in 1824. Sims became a surveyor for Stephen F. Austin's colony that year and continued to make surveys in Texas until 1858. In 1825, Sims married Sally Curtis; they had nine children.

Starting in 1839, Sims commanded several volunteer companies in a series of battles with native peoples. Some say that Sims was one of two men who founded the Texas Rangers.

In 1846, while on a surveying expedition to the Pedernales River, Indians attacked his party. He was the only survivor. By 1850, he was farming and ranching in Williamson County, where he died in 1864.

Robert McAlpin Williamson was born in Georgia in 1804 or 1806. When he was fifteen years old, he was crippled by an illness. His right leg was drawn back at the knee, and he was nicknamed Three-Legged Willie for the wooden leg he wore from the knee to the ground. He had his pants tailored accordingly. Williamson read the law during his illness and was admitted to the bar around the age of nineteen.

In the late 1820s, he migrated to Texas. He participated in the Battle of San Jacinto, for which he received 640 acres.

In December 1836, the Republic of Texas Congress elected Williamson judge of the Third Judicial District. The town of Columbus had been burned during the Runaway Scrape, so he convened the first term of District Court under a large oak tree. In 1840, he was elected to represent Washington County in Congress. He served in the republic's subsequent congresses.

He became legendary for his personal characteristics, his unique judicial decisions and his colorful way with words. He and his wife, Mary Jane, had seven children, one son being named Annexus.

In 1848, settlers in western Milam County asked the Texas legislature to create a new county, suggesting San Gabriel as a possible name. When the bill to create the "County of San Gabriel" came before the Texas Senate, it is said that Williamson stood up and excitedly protested having any more saints in Texas. The legislators created the county but named it after Williamson. He never lived in "his" county but often traveled through it.

After annexation, he served two terms in the Texas Senate, retiring in March 1850. He was an unsuccessful candidate for lieutenant governor in 1851. In 1857, his mind began to fail, and he died on December 22, 1859.

TEXAS "SWING"

Unlike many other Texas cities, Austin was never much of a lynching town. About sunrise on July 11, 1851, a slave called Lucky rode up to William Baker's dwelling, on Shoal Creek about one mile northwest of the capitol, and inquired the way to a neighbor's house. Baker invited Lucky to alight and wait until the family was done with breakfast. He did so. About this time, Colonel E.S.C. Robertson rode up on horseback and recognized Lucky as a runaway slave. He and Baker tied and placed Lucky in the north room of the house. Robertson left, intending to return in a short time. Soon after, Baker met Lucky at the door—Lucky had cut himself loose with a large butcher knife, which he had in his hand. As Baker attempted to subdue Lucky, he commenced stabbing Baker. Mathilda Baker ran to his relief, whereupon Lucky stabbed her in the chest, severing an artery and producing almost instant death. Baker was stabbed four times and died. Lucky fled on his horse. No one was present during the affair except the Bakers' five small children. Their screams brought several neighbors. Robertson soon returned and started up Shoal Creek on horseback. He came up with Lucky twice, but as he was unarmed, Lucky escaped.

A large number of citizens immediately armed themselves and went after Lucky. They found his horse and some of his baggage in a thicket the next evening, about one mile from the Baker house. The county sheriff offered a $200 reward for Lucky's apprehension and delivery, with the following description:

Black color; 6 feet high; weighs from 180 to 200 pounds; straight and well formed; intelligent looking; has a fresh scar in the forehead. He says he belongs to Col. Tom Moor, of Travis county, and that he was bought by him some twelve months since from a Mr. Storey, of Burleson county, on the Brazos River, for the last six months; and that his time having expired, he was then on his way to his master; that he had been lost, and wished directions in regard to the road; he states that he had a pass from Mr. Storey, but lost it in crossing high water.

Lucky was captured on July 26, discovered by a black woman, hidden in Judge Stephen Cummings's corncrib on Waller Creek. He was tried on the same day by a jury of twelve slaveholders in the statehouse, and his guilt being unquestionable to everyone present, he was executed in the presence of a large concourse of spectators, hanged from a limb of a hackberry tree, standing near where Colorado Street abutted the river.

"The owners of slaves indulge them to an extent not at all necessary to their comfort or enjoyment," the *Texas Gazette* complained. "Nearly half the negroes in town hire their own time, keep houses of their own, where no surveillance is over them, and which become pest houses to every neighborhood, where the most idle and worst disposed of this class assemble at night and discuss, if they do not organize, plans of mischief."

The other, and most spectacular, lynching occurred during the Civil War, with the three Willis brothers as the unfortunate guests.

Mystery shrouds their lynching. The only accounts are anecdotal; during the war, newspapers in Austin and elsewhere suspended publication for weeks or months at a time due to paper or ink shortages. Frank Brown, the most reliable authority on early Austin history, said the Willis lynchings took place sometime in 1864. An unnamed Austin citizen, in an 1884 *Austin Statesman* article, asserted that the lynchings were in 1863.

At any rate, there was a strong Unionist element in and about Austin in 1862 and 1863, stretching up the Colorado River into Burnet County and west into the Hill Country's German settlements, like Fredericksburg and Comfort. In the fall of 1863, Confederate soldiers scoured the countryside for renegade Unionists. It was in the context of these times that the Willis brothers were lynched.

The Willis family's reputation was anything but savory. There were six or seven grown men in the family, and according to one account, they were charged with being wholly responsible for the Cameron and Mason families' tragedy. The Willises had somehow ascertained that there was a considerable amount of money stored in one of these families' houses, and in order to get it, they went to a Comanche camp and persuaded the Comanches to assist in robbing and murdering these families. An eight-year-old girl from one of the families witnessed the event. She concealed herself when the Indians attacked, thus escaping death. When the attack was made on the house where the money was stored, a white man broke open the trunk and took out the money.

When news of the massacre became known, exasperated citizens assembled, arrested the suspected scoundrels and tried them. The little girl was brought forth as a witness. She stated a man with red hair and a sandy beard killed her mother and the Indians killed the rest of her family. Every prisoner who corresponded with her description was brought before her, one at a time. When Bill Willis was brought in, she sprang up, pointed to him and exclaimed, "That is the man who killed Ma, took Pa's money from the trunk, but Indians killed the rest."

Notwithstanding this strong evidence, the Willis boys were turned loose. They promptly stole a large number of horses and ran them to Mexico, where they sold them. While returning through the Hill Country to their home northwest of Austin, they were arrested on the frontier above Austin and turned over to the home guard company for safekeeping until they could be tried. They were charged with grave crimes, including inciting slaves to insubordination and assisting them to flee the country. The members of Austin's home guard infantry company were local citizens exempt from conscription but willing to perform military duty at home.

One lovely afternoon, the officer in charge detailed a sergeant and three or four privates to guard the prisoners; the other company members were absent, tending to their ordinary affairs. A mob quietly gathered, consisting of probably fifty men wearing no disguises, and took possession of the prisoners.

They conducted the prisoners to an open common about one hundred yards east of East Avenue, where three live oak trees then stood, about the center of present-day East Sixth Street. After the three brothers were securely tied, ropes adjusted around their necks and the ends thrown over a projecting limb fronting north, several strong men pulled them from the ground. The bodies remained suspended for two or three hours, after which they were cut down and buried in an unknown location.

"HOLD FAST WHAT YOU GET AND CATCH WHAT YOU CAN"

Anarchy struck Austin and the rest of the defeated Confederacy at the close of the Civil War.

When it became certain that the end had come, wild confusion ensued. Company after company of men came to Austin in search of the large amounts of quartermaster and commissary stores deposited around the city.

The scene beggared description. Crowds of soldiers collected in front of every government building, demanding the keys, and when they were not immediately forthcoming, forcible entrance was made and the grab game commenced.

The mania to "hold fast what you get and catch what you can" was not confined to soldiers. Men who had never taken any part in the war, together with women, children and slaves, assembled around the places where coffee, sugar, salt, bacon, rope, leather, cotton and so forth were dealt out with unsparing hand.

Individuals were seen going home loaded in the most grotesque manner. Here a man with a bale of rope in his hands and a string of tin cups around his neck; there another with two or three old saddles on his back. Here one with a can of balsam of Tolu; there another staggering under the weight of a heavy side of leather. Here a woman loudly vociferating to a black man to take a sack of flour to her house; there another who declared that her "brother-in-law had been in the war all through the thing" and she had never realized a cent from it yet. Here might be seen a small boy with his arms full of cotton cards and his pockets full of Epsom salts; there another bearing off in triumph a tin bucket full of quinine.

At the cotton warehouse, bales of cotton were rolled out on the pavement, the ropes were cut and everybody was invited to pitch in. Cotton was borne off by the sackful, armful, hatful, pocketful, by men, women, children and blacks, irrespective of services rendered in the Confederate army. Meanwhile, parties of men busily scoured the country in search of government mules, horses, wagons and so forth. Every quadruped having on him "C.S.," or in company with those having that brand, was seized. Woe to the luckless riding a mule with a Confederate cast of countenance. No matter if he was going to a wedding or funeral, for the doctor or to church, no difference if one hundred miles from home; the rider was dismounted and the beast conscripted at once. Wagon trains were stopped and the mules taken, the wagons left standing in the prairie.

These seizures were generally made without violence or noise, and the whole affair looked more like holiday sport than sober reality.

Meantime, the countryside was filled with direful rumors: Houston, San Antonio and other places were reported sacked and burned. The country was being laid waste. Large bodies of men were on their way, swearing vengeance against Austin. Sixty thousand Federals would arrive in a few days. General John B. Magruder was hanged.

Notorious gambler, pistolero and future Austin city marshal Ben Thompson was arrested for stealing forty-six sacks of coffee beans on May 25, 1865. He was not alone in his opportunism. The *State Gazette* reported on successive days:

> *May 25: Confederate soldiers, without officers or order, are coming in every hour, and there is nothing but plunder and sack going on, and the citizens are as bad as the soldiers.*
>
> *May 27: The town and all the adjacent country is in a dreadful condition. There is much looting and quarreling going on. It seems as if everyone had a claim against the Confederacy, and were paying themselves.*

By the first of June, everything was in confusion; there was no law. After unsuccessful attempts by citizens at maintaining order, Confederate veteran Captain George R. Freeman formed a company of thirty volunteers to protect Austin until Union occupation forces arrived.

The state's leading secessionists and most state officials had fled to Mexico or were getting ready to "light out."

One of the most spectacular—and unsolved—crimes in Texas history went down on the night of June 11, when the state treasury was robbed. Many versions of the crime exist, and one of the few details they have in common was that the treasury was robbed that night.

When news of the raid reached Captain Freeman, he and about twenty volunteers responded. By the time they arrived, a band of anywhere between a dozen and fifty-odd robbers were breaking into the safes. Freeman's men approached the marauders, who mounted their horses and fled toward Mount Bonnell, carrying with them about $17,000 in specie, more than half of the gold and silver in the state treasury at the time. They left one man behind who had stood guard. As Freeman's men approached the building, a brief gunfight erupted in which Al Musgrove and Fred Sterzing shot the guard, Alex Campbell, who was said to be drunk. Freeman was wounded in the arm. Campbell died the next day without confessing.

The state recognized Freeman and his volunteers for their service in defending the public treasury, but the legislature never rewarded them for their services.

ASSASSINATION IN THE MOST PUBLIC OF PLACES

The quarter century following the end of the Civil War was the most violent period in Austin and Texas history. Young Confederate veterans had returned home "full of piss and vinegar"—broke, disillusioned, cynical and ready to raise some hell, tendencies that often rubbed off on their younger brothers.

"Bound West" complained in the June 7, 1869 *Tri-Weekly Gazette*:

> *The young men are not coming up to suit me. They are not coming up with anything like educations. They are not coming up on the farms and in the workshops. They are not coming up with a solid thought in their heads. They are coming up too much about towns, where there is too much gambling, drinking and billiarding. They come up too much around balls, and horseraces, and tournaments, and cowdrives. They are coming up altogether too fast and too loose to promise good to their country or peace to society. They are too good shots with the six-shooter. The rims of their hats are too broad, and the greaser snakes coiled around the crowns of their hats look treacherous. The spurs dangling at their heels are several hundred times too large for civilization; but worse than all the rest, they don't read the papers. At my peril I lectured some of them, and I intend lecturing them and their parents. There is a power in these young men for good or for evil. Which shall it be?*

You were more likely to be lynched for rustling cattle or horses than for robbing or killing a man. No one, not even priests—much less elected high officials—was sacred to the thieves of the night.

Four game cow-pokers. *Solomon D. Butcher. Nebraska State Historical Society.*

Opposite, top: Cowboy dancing lesson. *Solomon D. Butcher. Nebraska State Historical Society.*

Opposite, bottom: A friendly card game. *Tarrant County College Northeast, Heritage Room.*

February 19, 1873, was one of the most anticipated days of the Thirteenth Texas legislative session: payday. That afternoon, House of Representatives Sergeant at Arms Rhodes drew $28,000 in currency and spent the rest of the day doling it out. By 6:00 p.m., he still had a little over $4,000. At about 7:30 p.m., he paid $260 in greenback $5 notes to Louis Franke, a freshman representative. While quite a number of legislators were on a junket to Galveston, Franke was fixing to go home to see his beloved family.

Franke was born in the German state of Mecklenburg in 1818 and earned a master's degree in law. Like so many other German intellectuals, he immigrated to the United States sometime between 1845 and 1847. Franke

"A Quarrel Over Cards." *Frederic Remington.* Harper's Weekly, *April 23, 1887. Public domain.*

served briefly as a Texas Ranger before joining the California Gold Rush of 1849. He returned to Texas in the early 1850s, settling in Fayette County, where he married Berhardine Romberg in 1853. They had six sons and two daughters. Franke taught music and ancient languages at Baylor College at Independence before returning to Germany in 1859 for treatment of a medical condition. He returned to Fayette County after a couple years, and in 1872, he won election as a representative for Bastrop and Fayette Counties in the Thirteenth Texas Legislature.

After receiving his pay, Franke left the representatives hall, as did Rhodes, who walked down the hall into the Senate chamber. Returning a couple minutes later, he was told that Franke had been attacked and robbed. Franke had apparently gone down the steps inside the capitol, passed round the building and, near the steps fronting south, was knocked down and robbed of his $260.

Franke fell at the bottom of the capitol's south entrance steps. *Public domain.*

Assistant Sergeant at Arms N.C. Reeves stated that he had passed up the front steps leading to the hall of the capitol building at about a quarter past seven o'clock and saw two large white men sitting together at the head of the steps, engaged in earnest conversation. About half past seven, a Department of Education clerk came into the hall of representatives and asked Reeves and others present if any of them knew a Mr. Franke, who was in a bad fix, down by the steps. Reeves hastened to the scene and found Franke sitting up; he said he had been knocked down and robbed.

Franke had recovered sufficiently to sit up but was not rational as he answered Captain William Sayers's questions as to who had struck him, saying it was a committee member. Colonel Nelson and S. Robb carried him to a friend's boardinghouse, where he died about half past four o'clock in the morning. He regained consciousness sufficiently to state that he had been attacked by two men he did not know. He was struck several times above the right eye with such force as to break the skull and drive it inward on the brain. One of his thighs was also broken, probably as he fell down the stairs.

J.T. Smith and Dr. U.G.M. Walker stated that they had seen two men standing at the spot where Franke was found; their actions were strange and mysterious enough to excite comment. Reeves was satisfied that they were the same men he had seen sitting on the steps but could not identify them because the darkness hid their features.

The next day, the House passed a resolution calling for better lighting at the capitol at night, and a joint House/Senate committee of three men from each chamber was appointed to investigate the assassination.

Franke's body lay in state in the hall of the House of Representatives, where services were held. Contrary to initial plans to inter his remains in the state cemetery, they were escorted from the capitol down Congress Avenue to the Houston and Central Texas Railroad depot for shipment back home to the family farm and burying ground at Black Jack Springs (near La Grange), where he was buried by an honor guard.

Franke's murderers, it was believed, intended to kill and rob Sergeant at Arms Rhodes. Franke was a person of similar frame and height as Rhodes, wore his beard somewhat similar to his and may have been mistaken in the dark for Rhodes.

The day after the tragedy, the *Austin Statesman* complained, "What has become of the proposition to light Austin with gas? If the city was lighted as it should be, assassinations could not be made in the most public places."

Within a week, two men, named Spain and Spalding, were under arrest for Franke's murder but were released.

Two weeks after his death, the legislature authorized the governor to offer a $5,000 reward for the arrest and conviction of Franke's murderer(s). With the investigation committee's failure to identify and arrest any suspects, the Texas Detective Agency's most expert private detective was engaged to investigate the case.

The legislature voted, with hardly a dissenting voice, to give Franke's family his pay for the entire session. The bill went to Republican governor Edmund Davis, who refused to sign it but let it become a law by constitutional limitation.

Democratic Party organs were quick to point out that he had signed a bill of a similar nature in favor of the family of J. Goldsteen Dupre, a black Republican member of the infamous Twelfth Legislature, killed by the Montgomery County unit of the Ku Klux Klan in April 1872, as he campaigned for Governor Davis's reelection.

Franke's widow refused a government pension.

Franke's murderers were never found, and robbery is believed to have been their only motive.

"KILLED IN THE LINE OF DUTY"

CORNELIUS FAHEY

Despite the advantages of bulletproof vests, helmets and assault rifles, being a cop is a dangerous occupation—always has been. That fact was first brutally brought home to Austin on Sunday night, March 7, 1875, between twelve and one o'clock.

The sharp peals of six-shooters and their flashes of fire, their deadly missiles belching forth—followed by a horse's hooves clattering on the hard street as the demon incarnate stole away—frightened and excited women, children and men as they sprang from their beds to the windows, doors and streets.

The general inquiry was—what is the matter? The question was soon answered: policeman Cornelius Fahey lay dying on a Congress Avenue sidewalk, shot through the abdomen. He was Austin's first policeman killed in the line of duty.

A stranger to town, a hard-looking case who went by the name of Mark Tiner, had refused to pay for what he called for at several saloons and drew his six-shooter as further assurance that he was not going to pay up. Mounting his horse, he fired a shot, and when Officer Fahey appeared on the scene, Tiner shot him. Fahey collapsed on the sidewalk, and Tiner galloped away up Congress Avenue, shooting at everyone who would dare to halt him.

City marshal Ed Creary quickly sent several mounted policemen in pursuit, accompanied by Deputy Sheriff Stokes and Fred Peck. When first seen, Tiner was walking, carrying a bridle in his hand, his horse having somehow escaped. By sunup, his pursuers numbered about twenty. They caught him in Hancock's

Congress Avenue toward the state capitol, 1870s. *Historic Houston Photographs, Special Collections, University of Houston Libraries.*

pasture, about three and a half miles north of the city (where present-day Hancock Shopping Center and Hancock Golf Course are located). He did not resist arrest, though he was armed with a six-shooter, which had been emptied of four of its shots. He was handcuffed and brought into town in a wagon. Before being locked up, Tiner was taken before the dying Fahey, who recognized Tiner as the party who shot him.

Tiner, who claimed to be a cattle driver from Rockdale, was of ordinary size, straight and slender, about twenty-two years old, with an illiterate daredevil look and small eyes. He had on a Mexican hat with a snake band, a jacket and dark leather overalls. He was not at all conversational but did admit that he had been on a spree the night before. His complexion was light, and Marshal Creary and others were of the opinion that his hair, which was dark, had been colored, done at a barbershop about a week earlier.

He closely resembled a man arrested a few weeks earlier, who claimed to be a cousin of the notorious Jim Taylor of the John Wesley Hardin gang. Some believed that Tiner was either Taylor or Hardin.

"Daredevil Look with a Mexican Hat." *From* On a Mexican Mustang Through Texas: From the Gulf to the Rio Grande, *by Sweet and Knox, Chatto and Windus, Piccadilly, 1884.*

Though shot through the abdomen, there was a hope of Fahey's recovery. But he died a few minutes after nine o'clock on the night of March 8. His funeral took place at the Catholic church, and Fahey's remains were conducted to Oakwood Cemetery on March 9 by the military band, the city police and Hibernians in uniform and many citizens.

Meanwhile, a great many people flocked to the jail to get a glimpse of Tiner.

"What a blessing it is that there is a place of punishment prepared for the consignment of earthly demons like he who shelled the city of Austin on Sunday

Times have changed since then. Now if a young man, who may never have visited San Antonio before, undertakes to shoot at the lamps, or indulges in any eccentricities of that character, he finds himself very much bewildered. Instead of creating admiration and awe, and being spoken of as a candidate for sheriff, as formerly, he immediately becomes such an object of pity that the spectators feel like taking up a collection for him. He is pulled off his horse and thrown down on the pavement by a couple of policemen. His pistol is ruthlessly taken away from him; and, while

one heavy policeman sits on his stomach, the other explores his pockets for more pistols. Then they put nippers on him, and lead him away in triumph to the lockup, without stopping to scrape the mud off his person. After he has spent a very disagreeable night, he is brought before the recorder to answer to the following high crimes and misdemeanors: disturbing the peace and quiet of the neighborhood, carrying concealed weapons, furious riding, resisting an officer in the discharge of his duty, quarrel-

A A 2

"On a Spree." *From* On a Mexican Mustang Through Texas: From the Gulf to the Rio Grande, *by Sweet and Knox, Chatto and Windus, Piccadilly, 1884.*

night and killed policeman Fahey," the *Statesman* declared. "But if there was no such place, it would be some satisfaction to keep them for life in the Travis county jail. In fact it is a question which is the most preferable place, Hades or the Travis county jail." Or they could be "cast into the Austin jail, where the atmosphere is so thick that it has to be hashed for breathing purposes."

For the past several days, there had been reports of several armed and desperate-looking men loitering about the city, insulting people after dark, flourishing six-shooters and making the night hideous. Tiner was but a fair sample of the lot.

"We often hear of armed men being seen in open daylight on the streets of the city and in the very presence of the police. Now, why are not such men nabbed the very moment they make their appearance?" the *Statesman* complained. "Citizens would prefer that a drunken, inoffensive man should stagger about the streets for half a day, rather than that a dangerous man should be allowed on the street armed for one minute."

Tiner waived an examination on March 16 and was committed to jail. His trial was set for July 15; Major William "Buck" Walton, the best and most expensive criminal defense lawyer of his time, defended him. Where Tiner got the money to pay him is anyone's guess.

The jury found Tiner guilty of manslaughter on July 21, 1875, and gave him five years in the penitentiary.

Author's collection.

Austin City Hospital. *Author's collection.*

By February 1880, Tiner was dangerously ill, such that the prison physician deemed it necessary to have him removed to the Austin city hospital.

Tiner died on Saturday night, March 21, in the city hospital. His body, accompanied by two men, was hauled to the cemetery the next evening and dumped out on the ground until a grave could be dug, buried as unceremoniously as if he had been a wild animal.

Sheriff J.T. Wilson

The threat of injury or death at the hands of desperados and other lawbreakers has always been constant to peace officers, but back in Austin's golden days of gore, they had reason to fear each other, especially when inebriated.

Austin was hosting the first training meeting of the Texas State Sheriffs' Association in January 1879, and lawmen from across the state had poured into town.

"The Social Glass." *From* The Rolling Stone, *by O. Henry. Doubleday, Page and Company, 1918.*

It was the rare peacemaker in those days who did not have a healthy taste for liquor. Then as now, getting souped up after a hard day of conventioneering was de rigueur. The more virtuous lubed up at the respectable saloons lining Congress Avenue while those with a taste for the low life slunk down to Guy Town.

And as Ben Thompson said, according to his biography, "Social ties brought the social glass—the social glass induced indulgence beyond prudence."

In a fit of imprudence, Marshal Samuel Ball, of Sherman, shot dead Sheriff J.T. Wilson, of Palo Pinto County, in front of the Branch Occidental Saloon at 708 Congress at about 11:30 p.m. on the night of January 24, 1879. Wilson and Ball had had some little difficulty earlier that day, and later that night, Ball and several friends were standing in front of the saloon when Wilson passed up the street. Someone in the crowd made a remark, whereupon Wilson pulled a pistol and advanced on Ball, saying, "Damn you, take it back," and fired three shots, one embedding itself in Ball's watch, one striking him in the finger and another missing him. Wilson was shot once in the breast, once in the back and four times in the side. Mr. Ellison, a cattleman, was accidentally shot in the hip.

During the inquest, quite a number of witnesses were examined, and all concurred that Wilson, who had been on a protracted spree, began the firing. Some testified that Wilson was passing along the street and that he stopped with his pistol in hand and advanced on the crowd in front of the saloon because a remark was made that he believed was intended to offend him, while others asserted that there was a quarrel going on in the crowd before the firing commenced.

A Mr. Wilson testified that Marshal Ball said, "I'm not armed, don't shoot," and that then Jim Lucy, a noted detective who later served as Austin city marshal, caught hold of the deceased and said, "For God's sake, don't kill that man." Lucy and Wilson, a witness said, then fell together on the sidewalk when several shots were fired at Wilson, but by whom, no one testified. One witness said that when the deceased fired his first shot, the crowd ran inside the saloon and that in a moment someone dodged out and caught hold of Wilson. A brief struggle ensued, and several shots were fired rapidly.

The verdict of the jury was that Wilson came to his death by pistol shots fired by Marshal Ball and others and that the killing was justifiable. Wilson was a Confederate veteran who settled in Palo Pinto County after the war. He became a Texas Ranger, rising to the rank of lieutenant. He was elected sheriff of Palo Pinto County in 1876 and reelected in 1878. He was about forty years old at the time of his death and left a wife and family to mourn his loss. In its roster of former sheriffs, the Palo Pinto County Sheriff's Office simply states, "J.T. Wilson…served until February 1879 when he died."

Ball met his own fate just a year later, shot on January 27, 1880, while attempting to eject a group of men who were creating a disturbance at a local whorehouse. He died on February 2, at the age of thirty-three. He had been Sherman city marshal for two years and also left a wife and family to mourn his loss.

"ARE YOU AS GOOD A MAN AS YOU WAS A WHILE AGO?"

Politics is a vicious game, always has been. Politicians today are always talking about declaring war on this or that evil, fighting for what is right and the like. But words don't kill anything but political careers. On March 12, 1878, Ninth Ward alderman Joseph Nalle used a knife to permanently settle his political differences with Fifth Ward alderman Thomas J. Markley.

Born in Culpepper, Virginia, Nalle came to Austin in 1870 and is said to have shipped the first trainload of lumber to Austin. By 1884, Nalle had lumberyards in Austin, Waco, Burnet, Stephenville and Alexandria, Louisiana.

Markley, forty years old and a native of Ireland, was a baker and grocer. Nalle was quite small while Markley was described as "strong, stout, active and athletic" and "as strong as two such men as Nalle," according to one of his best friends.

They had taken opposing sides on a proposition to appropriate money for building an additional city market house.

At the council's March 11 meeting, Nalle and several other aldermen submitted an ordinance for building a new $10,000 market house in Nalle's Ninth Ward, which Markley and several other aldermen opposed. Markley believed that the present city market at Hickory (Eighth) and Colorado Streets was sufficient. The opposing sides expressed "much feeling" that evening.

The *Statesman* sided with Markley, stating that the new market house appropriation was unnecessary and wrong.

Joseph Nalle. *PICB 06361, Austin History Center, Austin Public Library.*

Markley had told Joseph Hannig and others that he believed a group of men including Mayor Jacob DeGress and aldermen Radcliff Platt and Nalle were out to take advantage of the city, that they would "sell out their country and their God and their families for money."

On that fateful March Wednesday, Markley came into the *Statesman* editorial room just before 1:00 p.m. and was giving a history of the market house case in the council when aldermen Nalle and Platt and several other men came in. Fireworks began. Nalle called Markley a liar, and Markley replied in kind. Nalle grabbed a heavy inkwell from a desk and hurled it at Markley, following up with a pair of scissors, and was preparing to attack Markley with a chair when forced off by a bystander. When they finally laid into each other, Platt left a mark on the right side of Markley's face while Markley left Platt with a nicely decorated nose. They were separated, and Nalle went out into the composing room, where he remained until his companions came for him and they departed the premises. With Nalle out of the editorial office, Markley wiped the blood from his face, and a reconciliation took place between Markley and Platt. They shook hands. Markley said he had nothing against Platt, who was an old man whom he would not fight under any circumstances, and noted that they were both Masons.

Statesman publisher John Cardwell, who had been in the editorial room when the fracas began and then left, reentered the office, whereupon Markley apologized for his conduct. Cardwell accepted the apology and expressed a hope that friends would be made all around. Markley said that when he saw Nalle and they could have a talk, he thought they could reach an amiable understanding. Markley got up and left the *Statesman* office, remarking that he would "go down on the street and shave and feel better." Ten or fifteen minutes later, Cardwell heard that Markley was dead.

At the coroner's inquest, J.R. Cummings said that at about 2:00 p.m., he, Markley and a Mr. Gilleland were in conversation in front of the Palace Saloon, talking about the difficulty Nalle and Markley had had that morning over the market house question; at that time, Markley turned his head around and said, "There is Nalle now coming up."

Nalle was with a man named Odom, and they came up to where Markley and company were. Nalle seemed to halt.

Markley asked, "Are you as good a man as you was a while ago?"

Nalle answered, "I am."

Accounts vary as to whether Markley moved toward Nalle or vice versa, but they clinched, as if to wrestle, and while in that position, Nalle pulled out an open knife from the band of his pants and stuck it into Markley someplace near the heart. He then seemed to wrench and twist the knife as if he was trying to get it in Markley; he then pulled the knife out, and they separated. Markley put his right hand on the wound, stepped backward into the saloon and fell on his back, dead. Nalle wiped the blood off the knife on his pants, replaced it in his waistband and promptly gave himself up to the authorities. No weapons were found on Markley's body. The coroner's inquest revealed that Markley had been stabbed three times in the heart. There was no consensus as to the size of the weapon; some described it as nothing more than an ordinary pocketknife while others declared it resembled a bowie knife.

Public excitement about the killing was at such a high pitch that if it had not been for the prudence of a few influential men, mob violence probably would have resulted.

Markley was buried in Oakwood Cemetery on March 14 after a service at St. David's Church. The funeral procession was one of the most impressive Austin had seen, headed by the city police, fire department, Odd Fellows and Masons. Following was the hearse and a line of some forty-eight carriages and buggies. The doors of many business houses were closed while the procession was passing. Meanwhile, Nalle's preliminary trial was going on before Justice Fritz Tegener.

Being one of the richest men in Austin, Nalle immediately hired a "million-dollar" defense that included William "Buck" Walton. And like he did so many times for his friend Ben Thompson, Walton scored an acquittal for Nalle, after obtaining a change of venue for the friendlier climes of Williamson County.

Nalle went on to serve as Austin's mayor from 1890 to 1895 and enjoyed a robust business career, at one time living in Austin's second-most expensive home. It cost $40,000 to build. He died on the evening of March 18, 1911, at his home after a long illness during which he suffered terribly. He was seventy years old and left an estate valued at half a million dollars.

BIG BEN

Austin has had its share of larger-than-life characters, but no one even comes close to Ben Thompson. God broke the mold when he made Ben Thompson—a good thing, since Austin will never, ever be ready for another Ben Thompson, Austin city marshal from 1880 to 1882.

Bat Masterson said, "It is very doubtful if, in his time, there was another man living who equaled him with the pistol in a life and death struggle." The very name of Ben Thompson prompted "man killers," even those who had never seen him, to fly to safety.

Such was his reputation that contemporary accounts numbered his victims in the dozens. But Ben actually killed only a handful of men, unlike John Wesley Hardin. He did not rob trains or banks like Jesse James and Sam Bass.

One of the first things "Buffalo" Bill Cody did when he came to Austin in December 1879 to present his new play, *Knight of the Plains*, or *Buffalo Bill's Best Trail*, at the Millett Opera House was look up Ben Thompson. They went out of town with some other gentlemen, and Bill showed them a little crack shooting. With Thompson's rifle, he struck six half dollars out of seven that were thrown up. They had so much fun they did it again the next day. Unproved legend says that Ben accompanied Cody's troupe down to San Antonio, where he bested Bill in a shooting match.

No matter where he might roam—and he roamed a lot—Austin was home for Ben Thompson. No matter what the adventure, Ben always came home. Ben thrived on life on the edge, but he adored his family. They deserved only the best, cost be damned.

Ben Thompson. *From* Life and Adventures of Ben Thompson, the Famous Texan, *H.M. Walton, 1884.*

"Oh, he was such a handsome man. He was well groomed, wore red-topped boots that the ladies admired," Bettie Gilmer said in 1940. "It is often said that many women loved him. One day, he might be seen riding down the Avenue on a burro, dressed in buckskin and adorned with huge Mexican jewelry and an enormous sombrero. The next day he would be fitted out in the latest New York styles, wearing a Prince Albert and patent leather spats, a genuine dude."

Ben Thompson was a gunfighter. But he was so much more: gambler, gentleman, racketeer, Confederate soldier, mercenary for the Emperor

"Buffalo" Bill Cody, circa 1880. *Sarony, 680 Broadway, New York.*

Maximilian in Mexico, hired gun in the railroad wars, devoted family man, firefighter, lawman, drunkard, sentimentalist, dandy, aesthete, techno-geek, civil rights activist, philanthropist, philanderer and both pillar and scourge of his community.

His pleasant manner, his honesty and reliability in business transactions, his natural wit and humor, his unwillingness to take any unfair advantage of his enemies and his good looks caused him to be popular with men who abhorred his dissolute life and deprecated his lawless manner.

Gambling was Ben's chosen profession, but at the same time, he warned the youth of Austin of the dangers of following his path.

He was no ordinary murderer. Ambush was not his style. As a general thing, he allowed his opponent the first shot but never a second shot. On one occasion, it is said, he handed his enemy a loaded shotgun and directed him to go around the block while he, Thompson, went in the opposite direction. They met, and Thompson killed him.

Was Thompson's conscience troubled by remorse? Was he haunted by some of his victims? He went to plays at the local theaters, and his contemporaries regularly saw him listening to the remorseful ravings of Thomas Keene's *Richard III* and *Macbeth* with a most amused expression of countenance. No, remorse and fear were thoroughly foreign to his nature.

Ben shot up more gambling tables and streetlights than men. In Austin, he did precisely as he pleased, and the police only hesitantly attempted to arrest him, although he never punished any duly authorized officer of the law. He was always ready and willing to stand arrest, plead guilty and pay his fine, but under his own terms.

Thompson was born in Knottingley, Yorkshire, England, in 1843 and arrived in Austin with his family in 1851.

Ben's first shooting victim got a load of birdshot in his backside in 1857 for disrespecting Ben's father. Ben would scurry from one escapade to another for the next twenty-odd years until Austin elected him city marshal in December 1880. It was the zenith of his life. As marshal, he was the most respected man in Austin, a status to which he had always aspired.

He made the leap from Austin's pariah to its parvenu in four years. He had killed Mark Wilson on Christmas night 1876 at Wilson's Capital variety theater, seemingly in cold blood. Thompson and his gambling associates were annoyed that the Capital Theater was breaking up their business by drawing in their former clientele.

In the aftermath, there was something electric in the air that boded no good to evildoers. "Austin's best and most conservative citizens were seen to

"A Variety Theater." *From* Harter's Picture Archive for Collage Illustrations. *by Jim Harter.* *Dover Publications.*

shake their heads ominously and to say, with an air of quiet reserve that the present state of things cannot last much longer; if citizens are to be wantonly murdered, and the perpetrators go forth unwhipped of justice, then a more summary remedy will be invoked," the *Austin Statesman* warned.

There was much talk of raising a mob to lynch Ben. But they would have to deal with Sheriff Dennis Corwin first. Ben was staying at his place.

Ben's amazing acquittal for Wilson's murder didn't change Austin's lowly opinion of him or change Ben's behavior.

Between seven and eight o'clock on the evening of October 7, 1877, the *Austin Statesman* reported,

> *at a gaming table connected with the bar-room kept by Mr. Louis Maas, on Congress avenue, Mr. Thompson, feeling himself aggrieved at the treatment he had received the night before, allowed himself to violate the law by drawing his six-shooter and firing into the chips, checks, & c of the dealer of a game, which, it seemed, was played regularly in said house.*
>
> *General consternation prevailed, but was, to a great extent, allayed among the bystanders by the cool remark of Mr. Thompson that he would*

hurt nobody. After closing the game in this violent manner, Mr. Thompson quit the place and, two or three hours afterward, enjoyed the luxury of firing some fifteen or twenty shots in the lower portion of town. As no house was struck and no person injured, it is fair to presume that Ben was secretly, in his peculiar fashion, attempting to break the monotony of the evening.

So far as the city police were concerned, it appeared that, at the time of the shooting in the gambling room, Marshal Creary was in the northern outskirts of the city. On returning to his office, he was informed of the shooting in the gambling room. He at once inquired if any arrests had been made or if any information had been obtained as to who the party or parties were. Being answered in the negative, he directed his subordinates to proceed to hunt up and arrest the guilty party. Before this was done, Thompson had stopped his outdoor amusements and was enjoying himself indoors. Marshal Creary could not arrest him that night without forcing doors, and this he was forbidden to do.

When the police court met the following morning, Mayor DeGress called on Marshal Creary to state which officer was on duty on the avenue the night before when the firing was going on in the gambling saloon, and he stated that policeman O'Brien was on duty.

O'Brien, being called, stated that he was at supper when the firing took place in the gambling house and that he exerted himself to ascertain who had done the shooting but that not one word of information could be gathered regarding it.

The mayor thought it very strange that the police could not find out who did the shooting, when everybody else on the streets could learn without fatiguing themselves who did it. He then turned to the marshal and reprimanded him for not having had the guilty party arrested, and the marshal said that he had done all he could, that he did not propose to sacrifice his life or the life of any officer for nothing or for fun. The mayor replied that an officer should do his duty in preserving the peace and order of the city or resign, and he thought such lawlessness on the streets of the capital of Texas was shocking and outrageous. But Marshal Creary did not seem to concur in that opinion.

The mayor then inquired if the party had yet been arrested, and the answer no was given. An order for the arrest was then given, and the marshal instructed to place the party, when arrested, under a $500 bond in case the police court was not in session at the time. The marshal replied that a warrant for the arrest of Ben Thompson, charged with the shooting, had been placed in an officer's hand and that the arrest would be made under that warrant. In the course of half an hour, when the court was taking a recess, Thompson entered the building by the back steps, unaccompanied by an officer, and the marshal announced his presence. Ben Thompson being called, a paper was read to him charging that he had carried and discharged deadly weapons in a public place, endangering the lives of citizens and damaging property, contrary to law, to which charge a plea of guilty was made, and a fine of $50 and costs was entered against him by the mayor. This done, the court adjourned.

At the end of Ben's first year as marshal, four years after murdering Wilson, the *Statesman* sang a different tune: "Since his induction into office he has discharged his duties well. He has kept the city orderly, and to the best of his ability has endeavored to administer the affairs of his office faithfully and for the best interests of the public peace."

After a violent stint as a hired gun for the Santa Fe Railroad in its war with the Denver and Rio Grande, Thompson came home from Colorado in September 1879.

Once home, he determined to change his line of life to free his beloved wife, Kate, and their children from further anxiety about his personal safety. The election for city marshal was coming up, and Ben concluded to offer himself as a candidate. He consulted with some of Austin's best and most responsible men, who promised to support him.

After several years of lawlessness and frustration with what was perceived as a feckless police force, especially when it came to taming Ben Thompson, these "best and most responsible men" took a radical tack: "We need a city marshal and police force worthy of their titles. It has been said that every saint has a past and every sinner has a future. Perhaps this city could use a sinner turned saint for marshal. Could a sainted Ben Thompson be the answer to our prayers?"

And so, on October 2, 1879, Ben announced his candidacy.

His chief opponent was Ed Creary, the incumbent. Despite support from the press and the best and most responsible men, Creary whipped Ben soundly, 1,174 to 744 votes. Ben was disappointed but promised peaceable, quiet, orderly and law-abiding conduct.

It was a short-lived promise. The *Austin Statesman* reported on March 2, "Ben Thompson had a high old time in San Antonio Friday night and made things lively by firing off pistols on the streets. He was promptly fined $50."

"The best tempered and gentlest hearted people are sometimes ruffled by small things, and do quite wrong, though there be present no malice," Ben's biography explained. "In vino veritas is an old adage, and it might be

"Dealing Faro." *From "Out West on the Overland Train."* Leslie's Magazine, *Frank Leslie, 1877.*

said with equal truth that wine often compels the tongue to utter the deeper feelings of the heart."

After dining one evening with friends, Ben felt the effect of the champagne he drank and was in humor to catch fun on the wing. He and a friend went to the gambling rooms that belonged to Ben and his partner, Gus Loraine. Loraine was dealing faro. For some reason, they were not in exactly good humor with each other. Thompson believed that Loraine was cheating, so he pulled his pistol and shot into stacks of chips, scattering them in every direction. He also shot into the dealer's box, cutting it through and through, and, still not satisfied, fired at the chandelier, breaking it into a thousand pieces. Then he went downstairs into the keno rooms and, without saying a word, commenced to shoot into the "goose," which contained the balls with which keno is played.

As he ceased firing, he said, "This game ruins boys and shall be played no more." But he had no listeners. The men, boys, players, dealers, waiters and attaches of every kind had left through the doors or windows, down the stairs or onto the roofs of other houses.

He shot up the keno room over the Iron Front saloon early in the morning of April 21, 1880, and then retired for the evening. Later in the day, he turned out with his fellow firemen to celebrate San Jacinto day. While on the picnic grounds at Pressler's Garden, an officer informed him that complaints had been made against him, and he promised to call and settle the fines.

"After having any amount of fun," the *Statesman* reported:

Ben came back to this city, and about nine o'clock, discovered that festive little keno game "goose," and all in full blast, and as he had given orders for it to close, he of course was disgusted and again took upon himself the pleasing task of wiping it out if it took all summer. The boys who frequent the keno rooms till a late hour, and go home and tell their folks that the sick friend they have been sitting up with is much better, were sorrowful at the sight of Ben, and when he serenely asked for them to trot out their fighting stock incontinently fled in every direction. Some of them went out the back doors and some down the stairs into the saloon below, while a few of the night hawks spread their wings and went out the front windows. When Ben first appeared he cheerfully informed the whole concern that the game had to close, as he was the sole proprietor of the keno business in this city and didn't intend to have any opposition. Mr. I.S. Simon was in the house and was standing about ten feet from Ben, who drew his pistol, and pointing it at Simon, fired, and would have killed him, had not a Mr. Hines, standing near, pushed his arm aside, just as the pistol went off. After firing the shot, Ben left, and up to three o'clock had not been heard of. Two complaints were sworn out against him before Judge Lee. One of them charging him with assaulting Bob Holman and the other with assault with intent to kill I.S. Simon. There were also four complaints in the mayor's court.

Officer Sublett made the complaints against Ben, and notwithstanding he has been urged to withdraw them, he refused to do so. Ben Thompson had an interview with Simon and Holman the night before, and their difficulties were settled. That is, Ben Thompson settled them to his entire satisfaction,

"Crapping Out." *Lewis W. Hine, 1910. Photographs from the records of the National Child Labor Committee (U.S.).*

and informed the above gentlemen, it would be greatly to their interest to withdraw the complaints they had made against him. It didn't take them even two seconds to make up their minds, and they promised to withdraw the complaints made before Judge Lee. This coming to the ears of the witnesses on the charges before the mayor, they thought it would be to their interest to try and have the charges withdrawn there also, but the officers refused to do so.

It seems that Ben Thompson issued orders to the city police, that in case he became a little playful and used his musical pistol in making things lively, that they, the police, were to let him severely alone, and it seems they carried out the orders to a letter. On either of the nights he did the shooting he could have been arrested and on the night he was riding around the city he was seen by the officers and could have been arrested. A policeman was appointed on that night for the special purpose of arresting Ben, but hearing that he was riding around the city in a carriage and there being danger of his running afoul of them, the officer hurried home and went to bed.

Ben Thompson bought 16 copies of the Statesman *containing the account of his dispersion of the valiant keno crew and took the International*

"Playing Keno." *From* The Great South; A Record of Journeys in Louisiana, Texas, the Indian Territory, Missouri, Arkansas, Mississippi, Alabama, Georgia, Florida, South Carolina, North Carolina, Kentucky, Tennessee, Virginia, West Virginia, and Maryland. *Edward King. Illustrated by James Wells Champney. American Publishing Co., 1875.*

Roulette game, Reno, Nevada, 1910. *Library of Congress Prints and Photographs Division.*

A high-stakes game. *Library of Congress Prints and Photographs Division.*

Ben Thompson's roulette table burned in the great Bastrop fire of 2011. Pictured is a 1910 roulette game in Reno. *Library of Congress Prints and Photographs Division.*

train the next morning for Kansas. The officer heard he was at the depot and hurried with all dispatch to the rear of the capitol building to look for him, and continued the search until the train left.

From Kansas, Thompson again headed for Colorado before returning to Austin at the end of July 1880, evidently a chastened man once more, for nothing was heard of him until late November, when Sheriff Corwin, who had protected Ben after the Wilson killing, resigned. Marshal Creary resigned to take over the sheriff's job. Ben promptly announced his candidacy for city marshal.

On December 5, the *Austin Statesman* commented, "Mr. Thompson is well-known to the people of Austin. He is known especially as a man without fear, and there are very many here who regard him as the proper sort of a person to be marshal of a city like this one. They say his life may appear as a reckless one, but that his disposition is and always has been to act honorably to all men."

On December 16, Ben whipped his nearest opponent by 227 votes.

With this resounding victory, the *Statesman* publicly kissed and made up with Ben:

International and Great Northern Depot, 1880s. *Program of Events for 1973 Inaugural Festivities.*

The marshal has long lived in this city and is personally known to nearly all our old citizens and his reputation has extended into almost every state in the Union. His career has been an eventful one and at times has been marked by terrible encounters that have made him almost famous. He has an interesting family growing up, and of late has often expressed an earnest wish to settle down and educate his children. On the promises he made during the canvas just ended, many of the best and most prominent citizens buried the past and cast their votes for him. Such confidence in the simple promise of a man who has lived such an eventful life has rarely been equalled in the annals of this country; and, very certainly, has not been excelled. The members of Hope Hook & Ladder Company, accompanied by a large number of citizens, last night tendered to Ben Thompson a complimentary serenade in acknowledgment of his being elected marshal of Austin.

Ben, evidently, had quite a victory celebration, as the *Statesman* blandly noted on December 19: "Ben Thompson, marshal elect, is quite ill. As soon as he recovers he will qualify."

Two days later, he was "well" enough to take over active management of the Austin police department.

Once sober, Ben wasted little time in making good on his campaign promises, as the *Austin Statesman* reported on December 23:

> *There were eight or ten of them and along about the "wee sma' hours" yesterday morning they set about taking to the city. They were making an awful racket and from all appearances were determined to have a high time. Marshal Thompson was also abroad attending to official duties, and heard the above gents, and immediately getting on their trail came up with them just as one of the crowd calmly extinguished one of the street lamps. The marshal at once took in the situation and to the infinite disgust of the crowd bent on having a high old time, took them in.*

Once in office, the bark of Ben's pistol was seldom heard, as this incident recounted in the *Statesman* illustrates:

> *One day in April, 1881, a group of young men came to see the circus, and to have a little fun on their own. Along about 2 in the morning they left town on horseback, riding at a fearful gait. Ben happened to be standing on the sidewalk near the Raymond house and saw them galloping down the Avenue. He attempted to stop them, but two of them being on sleek horses managed to escape across the river. Officer Randolph followed them and fired a shot or two, hoping to bring them to a standstill. Ben hurried down and across the bridge, but being afoot, had given up the chase and was returning when he met the third member of the happy tea party, who was riding a slow horse. He was crossing the bridge with a drawn six-shooter in his hand when Ben ordered him to halt. "Who are you?" he said, his wicked-looking six-shooter gleaming in the starlight. "Marshal Ben Thompson, and if you don't surrender, it will be the most unhealthy moment of your life," Ben cheerfully responded. "Think so myself and to save trouble, and prevent anything like a funeral procession, I'll cave," the young man replied, and he was marched to the lock-up. The next morning his honor, the mayor, fined him $25 and costs for carrying a six-shooter.*

Ben simply was not afraid of anyone, no matter what their reputation.

Johnny Ringo was passing his time down in a house in the jungles of Guy Town (Austin's red-light district) early Sunday morning, May 1, 1881. Along about four o'clock, he missed his purse, and stepping out into the hall where some three or four of Austin's "nice young men" were seated, he came down on them with his little pistol and commanded them to "up hands" and searched them. Not finding his purse, he smiled beamingly on the young men and retired to his room while they quietly slid out and reported the facts to the police. Ben went down to the house but was refused admission to the room, whereupon Ben cheerfully kicked open the door and, to Ringo's infinite disgust, scooped him in. He was disarmed and marched to the station, and the next day he was fined five dollars and costs for disturbing the peace and twenty-five dollars and costs for carrying a pistol. Ringo settled with the city and left a wiser if not sadder man.

The Austin city marshalship allowed Ben ample opportunity to exercise his gentlemanly side, as the *Austin Statesman* approvingly noted during the winter of 1881: "Marshal Thompson had a detail of his gentlemanly police on the outside of the Opera House last night and they kept perfect order. They are a careful and polite set of officers, and few cities have their equals and none their superiors."

Ben put the fear of God into wrongdoers and publicly exhibited respect for the Lord God Almighty himself: he and his police force, in a body, attended divine services at Cumberland Presbyterian Church on Sunday night, May 22, 1881.

Thompson received a very handsome present from Buffalo Bill on June 14: a costly target pistol. The mountings were of gold and the handle was beautifully tinted pearl while the glittering steel barrel was most artistically and beautifully carved. It had engraved on the handle, "From Buffalo Bill to Ben Thompson."

But Ben could not help being Ben. At Turner Hall (which still stands at Seventeenth and Lavaca) on the evening of June 30, 1881, Ben and bartender Herman Lungkwitz had a few words. When Lungkwitz grasped a beer mug to hurl at Ben, Ben immediately drew a pistol and warned him not to do it. Lungkwitz didn't throw the mug.

Ben's bout of short temper was not surprising. His beloved mother was dying of liver cancer. She passed on July 10, at age sixty-six.

A large cortege of friends accompanied her remains from Saint David's Episcopal Church (which still stands in downtown Austin) to her grave at Oakwood Cemetery. The *Austin Statesman* noted, "Mrs. Thompson was a lady of more than ordinary intelligence. She was highly esteemed by all who knew her, and leaves several children and a large circle of friends to mourn her loss."

Ben mourned her sincerely, but his electric, rebounding nature could not long stay bowed, and he shook the cloud of melancholy away.

The evening after her funeral, Ben made one of his most novel arrests.

Lee County sheriff Jim Brown reached Austin from Louisiana, where he had been to arrest a man charged with murder. Brown had a sprightly looking deputy with him, whom suspicion, a few days earlier, as the couple passed through the city, intimated was Mrs. Amelia Schooman, formerly of Austin, and well known as "Mrs. Skeris." She was notorious in Austin for previously "dealing out the ardent." Her first husband divorced her for that behavior, and old man Schooman, her second husband, having discovered that she had too many lovers, left her to shift for herself.

When Marshal Thompson learned of the couple, he ordered his force to keep a sharp look out for their return and immediately report to him if they were to pass through Austin again. The evening after his mother's funeral, he learned that the couple, with a prisoner, had reached the city. Ben immediately repaired to the depot and, entering the car, found Brown's gallant deputy, armed with a six-shooter, guarding the prisoner. He arrested her and carried the whole tea party to the lockup, where Sheriff Brown furnished Mrs. Schooman proper apparel and gave bond for her appearance the next morning. She was charged with appearing in the streets in male attire and carrying a six-shooter. Brown explained he had her along to identify his man and work up the case so that he might make the arrest. News of her arrest spread like a fire, and people who wanted to get a look at the "small woman with such a big six-shooter" thronged the city hall corridors. She was described as having "sharp blue eyes, a small mouth, retrousse nose and a naïve manner, which made her quite attractive."

Sheriff Brown left later that day with his prisoner. His gallant deputy was not in the carriage on the way to the depot.

Brown was no shrinking violet. He was a flamboyant man, having one of the finest strings of racehorses in the state, racing some of them against the outlaw Sam Bass.

Brown also killed a number of men outright, which was not considered a bad thing, as the *Statesman* declared on May 11, 1876: "We admire the intelligence of the people of Lee County. They elect the right sort of sheriffs. Achilles was not more invulnerable than the sheriffs of Lee. The last one they created over there was shot last week and penetrated by nine buckshot but he still lives unawed, unterrified, and unkilled. His name is Jim Brown and they can't knock the black out."

Like an elephant, Brown did not forget, especially when it came to personal humiliation. At the beginning of September, Ben caught wind that Brown and some friends would attend the horse races that were to come

Cover, Life and Adventures of Ben Thompson the Famous Texan: Including a Detailed and Authentic Statement of His Birth, History and Adventures, *by One Who Has Known Him Since a Child. H.M. Walton, 1884.*

on September 3, with plans to create a disturbance that they hoped would draw Ben and kill him. Ben met Brown that day at the fairgrounds, informed him of what he had heard and said, if it was true, then was the time to settle the trouble, like men. Brown flatly denied the report, and matters were amicably settled.

Ben had found his niche in life. As his biography states:

His known nerve, his own innate sense of what was right in a legal sense, the chivalry born in him toward women, his appreciation and recognition of the dividing line between the lawful and the unlawful, caused turbulence, violence and disturbance to flee from his presence, and during his term of office no city was so free as was Austin from the thousand annoyances that are so common to all cities even of 10,000 inhabitants. While Thompson was city marshal, there was not a murder, not an assault to kill in the limits of the city; and as now remembered, not a solitary burglary, a single theft of any moment that was not detected, promptly brought to light and punished.

But Austin was by no means a chaste city, despite Ben's best efforts.

"Away up in a certain building on a certain street in a certain room certain orgies are carried on by certain young men with certain companions, that are observed by all in the neighborhood," the *Statesman* reported on July 30,

1881. "They are highly reprehensible, and if they are not stopped there will be trouble, and no end of scandals and such things."

His chivalry toward women had its limits: one evening in August 1881, Susan Billingsley, full of whiskey, was driving through the city at a fearful rate when she ran across Thompson. He stopped her mad career, but she refused to timidly submit to arrest and sailed into Ben; they had quite a lively tussle for some minutes. He finally succeeded in overcoming her, and she was fined ten dollars and costs.

Ben's biography neglected to mention that on several occasions during his tenure, he was the cause of several of "the thousand annoyances."

One day in May 1882, Ben was going out to Pressler's Garden and met a wagon with three men in it, which he said nearly ran into his buggy—he had to whip the horses in order to turn them and prevent a collision. He had John Hafner arrested for reckless driving, but when it was shown that Hafner was not the driver, he was released. Hafner swore out a complaint against

Pressler's Garden

The Austin Pleasure Resort.

South side Pecan street, ½ mile west of Hotel Brunswick,

H. KOPP, PROPRIETOR.

This beautiful Place of resort has recently undergone thorough repairs and is now one of the cosiest and most comfortable resorts in the city. The Garden is arranged with comfortable benches throughout, a fine dance pavilion, and its beautiful groves affording abundance of shade.

PRIVATE OR PICNIC PARTIES

Will find every convenience and comfort afforded them to spend their leisure hours pleasantly. Elegant lunches can be had at all times.

Dancing, Swinging, Croqueting and Games

Of various kinds may be indulged in with perfect quiet and safety from the intrusion of rough or improper characters.

Fresh Beer Always on Draught.

From Morrison & Fourmy's General Directory of the City of Austin, Texas, for 1881–82. *Morrison & Fourmy, Austin. Courtesy E.O. Wilson.*

Ben for cursing him. Deputy Sheriff Rudolph Krause was sent to arrest Ben, who refused to submit, remarking, "You go back and tell [Justice Fritz] Tegener when he wants me to send a gentleman for me."

Krause left and reported to his chief. Ben wrote Tegener a note in which he stated he would be down and would answer to the complaint. Tegener fined Ben one dollar and costs. Krause was relieved of his job.

As the annual city elections loomed large, the *Austin Statesman* declared on November 7, 1881:

> *The City of Austin never had an officer whose claims to re-election at the hands of her people rested upon a more solid basis than the record of duties impartially, faithfully and fearlessly performed, presented by Captain Ben Thompson. The city has been free from those disgraceful scenes which disgusted our people in times past. Rowdyism has been almost unknown, and his reputation alone has served to check excesses of those turbulent elements that have sullied the fair fame of the city.*

Despite overwhelming odds for reelection, Ben didn't leave anything to chance. He was an early believer in the power of advertising, and on the day before the election, the newspapers were littered with "spot ads."

"Ben Thompson never turns his back on a friend or an enemy, and has made Austin a good officer."

"The best people in Austin elected Ben Thompson marshal, and they will do it on Monday."

"Everything has been quiet for a year past and will continue so if Ben Thompson is re-elected city marshal."

On election night after the results were announced about midnight, an enthusiastic crowd accompanied by the Manning Rifles band visited Ben's home and serenaded him. A hearty good time prevailed. Probably too good a time, for reelection exacted a toll similar to his initial electoral triumph. "Captain Ben Thompson, city marshal, has been quite sick for several days. He is better and we hope he will soon be quite well again," the *Statesman* noted on November 16, 1881.

Two days after his reelection, some of Ben's friends presented him with a handsome black walnut office desk, exquisitely carved and elaborately ornamented in gilt. A comfortable and costly armchair accompanied the desk. It was just further evidence of the high esteem held for Ben by certain men.

The job of marshal kept Ben busy, but he found the time to tend to his considerable gambling interests. He did well enough to purchase an elegant sailboat in May 1882. He took a ride every evening or so and said that he could entertain his friends better in that way than in any other he knew of.

Ben didn't just collect prisoners; he also collected the finer things of life. He had the most interesting office in town.

"The city marshal's office is a perfect museum and art gallery," the *Statesman* declared on February 22, 1882, "but withal, there is nothing of the vapid aesthetic about Ben Thompson."

In April, Ben added a cabinet of minerals to the other attractions of his "studio" at city hall, as the *Statesman* described his office.

How did Ben Thompson become so wealthy? Tradition says that he was a successful gambler. However, some contend that he was not a particularly successful gambler but that he held a one-third interest in all the gambling establishments in Austin, which brought him hundreds, if not thousands, of dollars a week. In return, he protected them from any possible interference from legal authorities and any outside competition. The gambler who dared to establish a new gambling den in Austin quickly found out that he would either have to fight or pay Ben Thompson.

The world was Ben's oyster as the summer of 1882 drew nigh. The rest of Texas chastised Austin for giving Ben the high executive office of marshal, but the citizenry were not moved. They cheered Ben on his way in the line of duty, to the point that the *Statesman* declared in April 1881, "El Paso is in the care of roughs with six-shooters. They need a Ben Thompson as marshal."

Ben seemed invincible. It was universally admitted that he made an excellent peace officer. The lawless element knew with whom they had to deal and governed themselves accordingly.

But unseen storm clouds were gathering beyond the horizon, as Ben's biography states: during the time Ben was marshal, "there was peace; there was happiness; there was family unity, concord and content. But as in Paradise a serpent entered."

For some months Ben had planned to take his children to San Antonio to visit friends and pick up a prisoner. Having some leisure time and desiring recreation from his arduous duties, he notified the children that the time for the visit had come. Gladly, their mother prepared them to accompany their father on what was to them a gala day, full of sunshine, singing birds and blooming flowers.

They departed for San Antonio, where they arrived after a short ride on the railroad. He joined friends who were glad to see him, with undisguised and candid congratulation on his appreciation at home and his assured position among the better-thinking class of the people.

For a few hours, Ben enjoyed the association of friends. Social ties, unfortunately for Ben, brought the social glass, and the social glass induced indulgence beyond prudence.

There is reason to believe that the primary object of his visit was to settle an old gambling grudge against Jack Harris, proprietor of the Vaudeville Theater. Thompson had accused Harris of swindling him of diamonds and money in his gambling saloon adjoining the theater two years earlier, and Harris had threatened to kill Thompson since then. They had on previous occasions discussed his grievance with considerable acrimony. During one of these disputes, Thompson told Harris, "If you think I care a curse for you, just hop out into the plaza with your shotgun and see what I'll do for you."

Full of "the cup that runneth over," Thompson went to the Vaudeville Theater about 7:00 p.m. on the evening of July 11, 1882, and found Harris armed with a double-barreled shotgun, concealed behind a Venetian blind screen in the saloon fronting the theater. Thompson called on him to come out like a man, using some uncomplimentary language.

Harris replied, "Come on, I am ready for you." Harris was standing in a strong light and could be seen plainly. Thompson fired two shots through the blind; one struck Harris in the chest, passing through the lungs. On being shot, Harris walked upstairs to the theater, laid down the gun and fell. Medical attendance was called. He was conveyed home and expired within an hour. After firing his shots, Thompson made off, with the police in pursuit.

Harris's death produced a tremendous sensation in San Antonio. He was a power in politics, head of the gambling fraternity that ran the city and carried on its business without restraint. But Thompson had an abundance of money and powerful friends. He procured the best legal counsel, and they made every effort to set aside federal district court judge George Noonan's decision not to grant bail. Confined in the county jail, Thompson passed most of his time playing the banjo and reading newspaper comments on the killing. Thompson craved notoriety and pasted every newspaper mention of himself and his exploits in scrapbooks.

Ben tendered his resignation as city marshal several weeks after his arrest. Incredibly, the city council did not accept his resignation until October 23, after Ben had been refused bail by the court of appeals in Galveston.

People in other cities did not understand why the capital city of Texas had a well-known desperado as city marshal. It was, however, utterly incredible that while he awaited trial for murder, he should still be city marshal of Austin.

Ben's trial for the murder of Harris took place in San Antonio in January 1883, and against seemingly impossible odds, he was acquitted. But it was really no surprise—a man with friends and enough money could not be convicted of murder in Texas. Thompson had spent $65,000 (about $1 million in today's money) on his defense team.

Thompson returned home triumphant, and the champagne flowed. But the bloom was off the rose. He offered his services as marshal once more, only to be turned down flat.

How the mighty had fallen! Ben never recovered from his fall. His own hubris ambushed him.

During his last year of life, Thompson went to the dogs very fast, and well before his death he could hardly be called sane. In the last months of his life, he was drinking constantly, on the very verge of delirium tremens and acting more like a maniac than a reasonable being. Everyone was scared to death to cross him, and Austin started a deathwatch. During the last few months of his life, he had Austin so terrified that men spent their Sunday afternoons in the wooded suburbs taking target practice. The nearer he got to the foot of the hill, the more accelerated was his downward career, until he plunged beneath the dark waters of oblivion.

The death of Ben Thompson. *From the* National Police Gazette: New York, *1884.*

On the afternoon of March 11, 1884, Thompson, in the company of noted pistolero King Fisher, took the train to San Antonio, ostensibly to see Ben's favorite actress, Ada Gray, who was appearing in *East Lynne* at Turner Hall. Ben had been drinking all day and evening and, after the play, decided that they should visit the Vaudeville Theater, run by Jack Harris's business partner, Billy Sims, and Joe Foster. From the moment he entered the Vaudeville, he was a doomed man. The quartet inevitably met, and unpleasantries were exchanged, Thompson accusing Foster of having once cheated him out of money and jewelry while gambling. As they stood near the door, Thompson again denounced Foster as a thief and drew his revolver, at which time firing from both sides began. When the smoke cleared, Fisher and Thompson lay dead, and Foster a'dying.

The next day, the corpses of Fisher and Thompson were shipped to their respective hometowns for burial. Austin physicians performed an extensive autopsy and concluded that Thompson and Fisher had been ambushed from above by a concealed group of armed men.

Austin took him back with full honors, all past transgressions washed away. He enjoyed a huge funeral and was buried next to his mother in Oakwood Cemetery.

"MY AMEN IS HAPPINESS TO COME"

In the city of weird, Professor Adolphus Ernst Damos was the most eccentric creature to ever wander the streets of Austin. Hands-down. No contest.

Austin has always been the capital of weird in Texas; it had poets, piano players, a museum, a debating society and a library before it had a proper saloon or a prostitute.

Austin became home to the state's first lunatic asylum in 1858, and the people of Austin took the asylum's inmates into their hearts. The cream of Austin society attended the balls frequently hosted at the asylum, and at one fête in the 1890s, the lieutenant governor fell victim to an elaborate joke. Although a rotund man, he was light on his feet like Jackie Gleason. He considered himself a ladies' man, and as he tripped the light fantastic, flitting from one beauty to another like a social butterfly, a friend approached one of the comely young ladies as yet untouched by His Lieutenant Excellence and warned her to be careful when the festive fatty approached, for he was one of the asylum's inmates. When he inevitably bore down upon her, he was surprised by her singular resistance to his charms. Deflated, he slunk away and brooded until informed of the practical joke played on him.

Adolphus Ernst Damos was an Austin fixture for decades. He said that he first came to Austin in 1850. During the Civil War, he lived in Marshall, and in 1865 he returned to Austin, where he lived until his death.

Proudly Prussian, he was in early life distinguished for intellect and learning, a highly educated gentleman who left his family in Europe to come

DAMOS FOR GOVERNOR.

From Sketches from *Texas Siftings, Sweet and Knox, S.W. Green's Son, 1882.*

to America to establish himself. He met with success and sent for his family. They embarked, but their ship never arrived and its fate was never known. The shock and grief largely destroyed his mind. He could not believe that his family would not come. He gathered and read every available paper, looking for some news of them. While trudging the streets and sifting the trash dumps and while sleeping, he held his collection of newspapers spread out, placed against his breast and held in place by his folded arms. He never abandoned hope.

At times, in his comparatively lucid intervals, he showed in conversation that he was the intellectual equal of men whom the world recognized as leaders in society and state affairs. He took a deep interest in the Franco-Prussian War, and early every morning, he sought the papers to learn about the great conflict's progress. Nothing pleased him better than to get hold of one of the great dailies containing maps of the war, and for hours he would pore over it, studying the locations and movements of the vast armies. He was the best posted man in Austin as to the topography of the country in which the armies were concentrated, the distance between important points and the facilities for communication between the same. The great German victory delighted him to no end.

Charity fed and clothed him, and day and night, in sunshine and in rain, in winter's storm and summer's heat, he tramped around and, like the eccentric but brilliant writer Samuel Johnson, touched nearly every post in the streets through which he passed. He slept wherever a sheltered place offered itself. At night, along about ten or eleven o'clock, Damos could be seen seeking an open office, and if none was found, he slept on the corridor or the upper floor of some of the large business houses. He was fond of beer and made daily visits to all places where the beer kegs were set on the sidewalks, and from them he drained the last drops. The bartenders kindly left enough of the beverage in the kegs for the professor to drink and treat his friends. He went through the ceremony in grand style.

His chief diet was said to be raw mackerel, rotten apples, kraut and limburger cheese, and his occupation was reading and toting his papers about and stealing as much as he deemed necessary to maintain his lifestyle.

Damos often got drunk as a "biled owl" and cavorted about like a wild mustang. One night, Sheriff Dennis Corwin took hold of him to quiet him, but he would not quiet; on the contrary, he fought like a tiger, and it took three or four men to subdue him. He had filled up on sour beer and was badly "off."

The professor did not have to be drunk to go off like a shooting cannon. One unpleasantry occurred in 1873 between Damos and one of Austin's rising lawyers. Damos, conceiving himself insulted, stopped and, asking neither for an apology or explanation, went for the legal gentleman, fully determined to use him up. The lusty appeals of the bottom man in the fight brought timely intervention, which happily prevented what promised to be a very serious affair. Damos was pronounced to be "something" in a fight.

Damos's surviving literary legacy is sparse—a trio of letters written before the Civil War to Governor Hardin Runnels—but they speak to the depths of his insanity. One of them, which asks for a variety of favors including resources to open a school and a good-looking young virgin for a wife, follows, transcribed exactly as written:

Jefferson, Cass County, Texas
October 27th, A.D. 1859
One copy to the Notary Public, Jefferson, Texas

Governor Excellence
A commonly communication for my petition for this season Legislature house and senate I you ~ you I herewith pray for commonly praying me nothing in the way today to be commonly right citizen a resaid entitled of and pray herewith to you and said season Legislature house and Senate.
1. Resolved that to read is in my accomplishments several a petition commanding commonly for Relief. Relief for Adolphus E. Damus, Professor of Agriculture and Chemistry.
and Relief for Adolphus E. Damus, Esquire
and Relief for Rev. Adolphus E. Damus, Jefferson, the state Texas. One inhabitant at praying relief. I say that to read is instead entitled to read and read entitled and Entitled and as the case may be so testified that I have got, the commoner officialment.
entitled at his office 17th September 1859 at his office W.M. Freeman, Esq. at his office Notary Public office—Jefferson, Texas. Became a Rev. at his office official by A.N. Corkle, supt. For A.T. Society in Texas, etc., etc., etc.—as aforesaid above mentioned at all my accomplishment, accomplishment for my position thereupon. Amen.
Rev. Damos is a Lutheran church and school, said church most rites Episcopal church, Holy Bible, preaching, teaching thereon.
My amen is Happiness to come
My Jesus is just right
My Jesus is the right judge
Canon law in honor the common law and his word upon it, honor the law of it land in which you leave.
Thereon
My prayer
Make me up for a good habeas corpus viz homestead viz bona fide a actual bona fide subscriber for the commonly support

I ask you
Each year a copy or a examplar
One State Times
I ask you for it each year the commonly support the State Gazette and his reseason newspaper
I ask you the commonly support of government books
Thereon,
~ that me not ought to ails of your books,
~ that me not ought to ails any of your maps,
~ that me not ought to ails any of your atlases
~ that me not ought to ails any of your prints and sketches
~ that me not ought to ails any of your instruments, in this case special.
I ask you a telescope propose ~ engineer books and instruments
And I ask you of all good comfort for a library I her proprietor thereon.
And I ask you prepaid by the state prepaid prepaid has freight prepaid. Prepaid her postage, prepaid all costs to bring me all prepaid to my living place or as I may order for it at.
~ I ask you a hill for a building a edifice to have the commonly roof over it. I ask you the money coined monies for to build said edifice.
~ I ask you a hill for at in this county if possible in the middle of this county, at a hill for library edifice and has vicinity, a learning place, a commonly learning place, surrounded said library edifice and the means of it as coined money and
I ask you a water well, drink water and offer again too a artesian well to health it country and I ask you all well-wishing too to all commonly rigth Authorities for said undertaking for said enterprise.
And I ask you a annual librarian payment $3000 three thousand dollars payable in portion at the 12th part at each month one twelfth
And I ask you for now $1000 thousand dollars for my propriety costs prepaid. Amen.
And I ask you a healthy place for said establishment a library bibliothak. I am the principal thereon and what I can do for it a librarian commonly librarian—Grand Lecturer honor me some of it. Amen
sustained my will by twelve hundred time twelve thousand right citizen the revelation upon it before
said said Jesus
12,000 angels, 12,000 romish jewish citizen. Amen.
Trustings, willness I pray.
Such opinion as was on the right side,

Other opinions was on the left side
In the middle was it right judgment between both.
The middle the judge, the middle the state's attorney reading the law.
The right Judge judgment honor the jury ~ men ~ the jury the commission the right jury. Amen.
It is him by it country sustained is.
Chiefly sustained. Then will he gain nothing in the near term? Thereon nothing in the near term? I herewith pray Amen.
A valid voucher. Amen.
This my petition a voucher. Amen.
This my petition a valid voucher. Amen.
What are trustings?
Conversation, situations in right health, mannerly—citizenships, her trusted right, her constitution ~ further her legislature ~ her house ~ her representatives, her Senate and her members of Senate (in olden time Senators her citizens) rigth wife of rigth citizen—pray we, Amen.
Witness further:
I am, that is, Adolph Ernst Damus, author and proprietor of this accomplishment for my petition.
I am is, A.E. Damus, (39) thirty and nine years old, in my tenth year in Texas
~ abide with you all the term ~ your eighteen years education and your twenty-one year education aforesaid
~ twenty-one years aforesaid
~ and have that heard to be a man
and have that heard to work at wife;
and have that heard to lay before you my wish thereon wish and wishes;
I ask by your care, as the case may be, a daughter of a good house, virginity, education, ~ if possible daughter of the member of the Senate of a Holy Bible Family, her father. She shall have healthy limbs, black brown hair, head, hair ~ brown pupils her eyes
fine build her figure, my body fine built. She same circassian complexion. Her endowment not a poor one. She my wife. I her husband. I am not without hope upon it.
Pray only? But I will have! Amen.
I am not without hope upon it.
~ pray so
A.E. Damus
give me your help thereon

160 for 160, or least number of acres; 166, mediated number is 666 acres, commonly number at 1200 acres. Large number of acres so many as you can add. Amen.

pray you

She commonly ask for it

She commonly praying for it

She commonly accomplishment for the petition of it,

Respectfully, yours truly

A.E. Damos

~ ameliorationable

this accomplishment for petition

~ do more the commonwealth one portion to me aforesaid prayed she and me.

Twelfth

It tenth year in Texas

Preaching the word of God

Without cease of God.

There was much pity for Damos but also much complaint.

One month, it was: "Why is not something done with Prof. Damos? He is in a filthy condition and no doubt covered with vermin. He should be looked after at once. We do not know who is the proper person to do it, but it should be done."

The next month, it was: "Professor Damos must go!"

Until the old limestone "colonial" capitol burned down in November 1881, he passed many nights in the building, and its loss was a source of much trouble to Damos, who then passed his nights in the corridors of the Brueggerhoff building. During cold nights he suffered a great deal, and it seemed it would be an act of charity to provide some place for him. Indeed, in view of the fact that he was growing worse and was at times now really dangerous, most folks thought it was time for the authorities to have him placed in the asylum.

Little girls and boys were warned to give Damos a wide berth when they met him off the main thoroughfares, for it was feared that should he get his hands on them, he would surely inflict terrible injuries, if not kill them outright.

A few days after the capitol burned, he caught a little boy and might well have murdered him had not a gentleman been passing and rescued him from the old man, who had been worked into a perfect frenzy by being hooted at and teased.

Another evening, Damos became so enraged at a street urchin who indulged in a little raillery at his expense that he struck the boy a pretty severe blow with his fist. If an officer had not arrived promptly, it is pretty certain that the boy would have been badly beaten. Damos was locked up until morning, in the belief that the city refrigerator would cool him off.

Damos was then discharged from custody after being thoroughly washed, shaved and clothed in a brand-new suit of duck. Because boys regularly, wantonly, cruelly teased and tormented the old man, the authorities concluded that Damos was justifiable, or at least excusable, in protecting himself.

In September 1884, Willie Claire was placed under bond for disturbing the peace of old Damos by pushing him off the sidewalk.

Damos occasionally did some mischief by disturbing books and papers in the different offices, and frequently he carried off little things. But mostly, he stole or otherwise accumulated clothing, particularly overcoats. One day, he stole a coat valued at sixteen dollars and three dollars in postage stamps from the office of a lawyer named Hill, who found his coat on the back of the thief and made Damos give it up.

Those who were fortunate enough to own overcoats had to keep an eye on the eccentric wanderer whenever he developed a penchant for the above article. He took one from the offices of a certain gentleman one December day in 1880. It was discovered under some five or six others the professor had on and was returned to the owner, who was left wondering on the quantity of disinfectants necessary to purify it.

Damos started his summer campaign a few months later by stealing the clothing of Jim Whitis, a person of color who was a porter of the federal courtroom, and four or five dollars in the pockets.

He was not especially discriminating in his acquisitions. On one August dog day, he was proudly showing off a lady's nice gray woolen shawl, as good as new, wrapped up in his papers.

Austin predicted the weather by him. As the mercury went up, Professor Damos longed for an additional overcoat. Just as March showers bring April flowers, whenever Damos was seen wearing an extra overcoat in May or early June, Austinites knew they would enjoy hot weather for the rest of the season.

Damos, having many of the peculiar habits of Dr. Samuel Johnson, wore three coats and as many pairs of old pants during the hot weather. Besides these comforts, he wore two or three old hats chucked into one another and bore before his bosom his package of ten to one hundred well-worn newspapers. When asked why he was so warmly clad, he said the good people of Austin had plenty of clothes and things to give away when nobody needed them but that he was glad to get a single coat in winter. Having three he was forced to wear them, since he had no place of deposit and no frau to take care of them.

Once he put them on, he did not take them off. That task was left to others. One August afternoon, firemen held Damos over an open fireplug. Captain M.D. Mather applied a double force of steam, and a great stream flowed into the river. The wrecks of sixteen suits were slowly washed away, and Damos lost fifty pounds in as many minutes. If they had reached the bottom of those old suits, they would have found some that dated back to the days "when Edmund J. Davis was king of Texas and Damos the philosopher of his cabinet."

Damos's cleanings occurred once or twice a year and always in August.

After his August 1884 cleaning, the *Austin Statesman* noted, "Old Professor Damos, the non-cosmoposmentis of Austin, was washed and shaved and his hair cut by the county and dressed in a new suit of clothes today. He was so proud that for the first time since the steamer went down with his family he put down his papers and strutted around with his walking cane."

The professor was a leading source for local jokes.

One night during the Christmas season of 1874, a full-mask party took place at Major Dewey's, about twenty couples being present. One of the maskers personated Professor Damos perfectly, making much merriment for those present.

"Things are getting better economically," the *Statesman* joked in January 1879. "Even Damus has money. He subscribed for the *Statesman* yesterday and paid in advance for one copy."

"When old Damos is no more, the weeping world will say another landmark is gone. He totes around many acres of the country."

"A new planet was discovered by a professor of astronomy, well known to the citizens of Austin, last night. The planet was of a bright red color and appeared directly east of the Avenue, and was attached to the tail of a kite that some boy over about East Avenue was flying. The gentleman who discovered said planet is well known under the nom de plume of Professor Damos."

"Who says the rights of the colored man are not respected? Only a day or so ago a contract was let for washing 'Professor' Damos. Both bids were the same, but the colored man got the contract over the white competitor."

The professor would rightly go on to enjoy state and national fame and infamy.

Governor Oran Roberts's friends got very indignant at a cartoon image of Damos (the only known image of him known to exist), probably because it also resembled Roberts. It headed *Texas Siftings*'s formal endorsement of Damos as the state's Democratic candidate for governor in 1882:

> *If Governor Roberts persists in refusing to become a gubernatorial candidate for a third term, we beg leave to suggest to the Bourbon Democracy of Texas that they consider carefully the claims Prof. Damos, of Austin, has on the party.*
>
> *The professor is a crazy man who has for years been going around the streets of Austin carrying in his arms a bundle of newspapers. He lives on charity and the draining of beer kegs.*
>
> *Like many of the gubernatorial candidates, whose names have been suggested, Professor Damos is entirely unknown outside of the town in which he lives. This appears to be an indispensable qualification of the Texas gubernatorial candidate this year, hence it becomes necessary that we should inform the people of Texas of the manner and habits of the man who is worthy to succeed Governor Roberts, and carry out the policy of the Bourbon Democracy of Texas.*
>
> *In the first place, the great qualification of Prof. Damos to carry out the Roberts philosophy is that he is hopelessly insane. In carrying out the Bourbon policy he has the advantage over Roberts that he never changes his mind. Roberts changes his mind continually, although the change is not always for the better. He has changed his mind about free schools and immigration. He has occasional lucid intervals. No man who changes his mind in the least or has a single lucid interval, is worthy of being the standard bearer of the Bourbon Democracy of Texas. Professor Damos never changes his mind, and he would not know what a lucid interval is if he were to see a dozen of them. In fact, Damos has no mind to change, hence as a representative of the party he has no equal. Why the Texas Bourbons have not displaced Roberts and made Damos their standard bearer, years and years ago, is utterly incomprehensible to us. Damos is more in harmony with the traditions of the party, and less contaminated with modern heresy about free schools, protection to life and property than either Roberts, Ireland, Coke or any of the would-be Bourbons who are aspiring to be somebody in the party.*
>
> *But to return to Professor Damos—the coming man. There is nothing the true blue Bourbon Texas Democracy detests as much as style. Plug hats, clean shirts, stylish clothes and dignified manners savor of aristocratic*

inclinations, and are calculated to undermine our republican institutions. This being so, Damos is the man to save the country. His clothes are in such a condition that they would have to be washed and repaired before they would be fit to throw away. In summer he frequently goes without shoes and stockings, and he is much given to picking up cigar stumps out of the gutter, and enjoying a quiet smoke in a back alley. He never washes, and could not identify a piece of soap if he were to see it. Governor Roberts has of late years departed from Democratic traditions by dressing up in a tolerably presentable manner, although his hair needs trimming right now. If he keeps on, and he usually does keep on, he will be little better than an aristocrat like Arthur, hence the election of the people will be made with Damos than with Roberts.

Governor Roberts is very accommodating in signing pardons, thus giving expression to the natural sympathy the Bourbons have with the criminal elements of society, but Damos will sign anything. He would turn out all the convicts, which would add greatly to the strength of the party, which action would also be in harmony with its record in the past.

When it comes to literary attainments, Roberts has nothing to brag about over Damos, although it must be admitted that as an idiotic production, Governor Roberts' book on Texas is a pretty strong card. It is also true that an Alabama university has conferred the L.L.D. on Roberts, thereby creating him a doctor, but Damos is a professor, and a professor is somebody in this country. Played-out music teachers, corn doctors, and sleight-of-hand performers are professors, hence we cannot see why Roberts should put on airs to Damos on account of the Alabama title of L.L.D.

The great object of having governors at all, is to supply the coming Texas University with professors, and Professor Damos, after he has got through being governor, will probably be made Chancellor of the University, provided that Roberts does not already occupy that responsible position. Judging from the kind of material we have heard spoken of his connection with the proposed University, it will be a great act of condescension if Damos accepts any position, even the highest in the institution.

If, however, the Democratic opposition overlooks the claims Damos has on the party, we hope Damos will run independent. Unfortunately, like several other prominent Democrats, being out of his head, he has not got sense enough to pursue that course.

Siftings also used Damos to lampoon the legislature, which it did in almost every issue:

There is a half-witted old fellow in Austin called Professor Damos who wanders about the streets, holding a lot of old newspapers in his arms. Max Dinkelspiel stopped Prof. Damos on Austin [Congress] Avenue yesterday, and asked him if he did not want to go to the opera house, where the legislature is in session, and be introduced to the members. The old man shook his head and said he would go some day when he had his old clothes on.

"Why do you want to put your old clothes on when you go to see the legislators?" asked Dinkelspiel.

"Because," replied Professor Damos, "If I look right shabby they won't think I'm putting on airs on account of my mental superiority over them. I want to flatter them."

Despite the *Siftings*'s claim that "Professor Damos is entirely unknown outside of the town in which he lives," Damos was in fact, already one of the most famous "characters" in the country. It's just that no one knew it.

One of the country's most popular theatrical works of the 1880s was John A. Stevens's melodrama *Unknown*. Stevens, an actor/playwright, equally well known for *Passion's Slave*, played Austin regularly.

Stevens and a good supporting cast presented *Unknown* and *Passion's Slave* at Millett's opera house in November 1882.

A large and very appreciative audience greeted him on his appearance in the title role of *Unknown*. His strong delineation of the unfortunate and insane Harold was followed with interest through five admirably constructed acts, each of which closed with a strong situation.

The opera house "was filled to witness the superbly artistic rendition of this most popular character, Harold," the *Statesman* critic wrote.

We frequently heard the expression as the audience dispersed: "That is the best acting we have seen in that house this season." At all events the audience was captivated and insisted on calling him repeatedly before the curtain. The applause at times was deafening and the interest never flagged for a moment. The support was very good in most particulars. "Jack Salt," by Mr. Theo. Hamilton, was the finest bit of character acting we have seen in that line that can now be recalled to mind. The scenery was magnificent and the stage effects very realistic.

Imagine our surprise when we found out several days later that Professor Damos, the literary wanderer of Austin…was the original of John A. Stevens' "Unknown." When that actor was here, some seven years earlier, he was casting about for the materials for a new play. He saw the professor and made inquiries about him, which finally led him to construct the play, which for more than ten years was successfully produced throughout the country.

Stevens never gave Damos a dime in gratitude, nor any recognition beyond what he told the *Statesman* critic.

Like General Eisenhower, who was courted by both major political parties for the U.S. presidency in 1952, the *Statesman* endorsed Damos as the ideal Republican candidate for high state office in August 1884:

Yesterday Professor Adolphus E. Damos, Col. W.Y. Leader's candidate for Comptroller, severed his connection with the newspaper business, for the present, in order to devote his entire time to the management of his interests in the coming campaign. It is understood that the Republican convention of Travis County will pass a resolution endorsing Professor Damos' candidacy, and in the event it is decided by the state executive committee of the party to hold a state convention, there is little doubt but that a solid Damos delegation will go up from Travis. There is one thing certain, and that is that no more suitable man for the high office to which the professor aspires could be found in the ranks of the Republican party in Texas. In fact, he is a typical Republican. His motto is to secure everything in sight, and look out for more.

In national affairs the professor is entirely in harmony with the platform of the "bone-hunter," as enunciated at Chicago. He is more thoroughly versed upon the subject of the tariff than any man, perhaps, in his party, Judge Rector not excepted. On the matter of national banks, his conduct yesterday showed him to be thoroughly in accord with the attitude of his brethren throughout the land, for, after being dressed up a la dude, by Sheriff Hornsby and given a walking cane, he strolled into the First National bank, and with that nonchalance for which Republicans candidates are so noted, proceeded to buy a voluntary "assessment" upon the institution. The bank president bolted, however, and it is now rumored that Professor Damos will use his influence at Washington to have the establishment suppressed. Comptroller Swain is at present absent from the city, but has been apprised of the fact that there is a new "Richmond" in the field.

Damos was sufficiently well known when, in March 1885, *St. Louis Globe-Democrat* correspondent Tobias Mitchell came to Austin to report on the city and the doings of the legislature (which was then in session). Late issues one day of the paper contained burlesque pictures of legislators, with short descriptions of each man. The likenesses included Alexander Sampson (the Senate's calendar clerk), Damos and other noted Austin personages. Sampson was not at all pleased with his sketch, only a rear view being presented, and his ill temper was remarked upon by a good many, who, while having an equal or greater right to complain at the artist who pictured them, nevertheless laughed off the matter in the humorous way in which it was intended.

Between ten o'clock and eleven o'clock that night, Sampson and Mitchell met on the sidewalk near the Avenue Hotel. Sampson told Mitchell that the paper had given him a rough deal and cursed the man who did it in a way that no living man on earth with a spark of manhood about him ever fails to resent. At this, Sampson said Mitchell drew a knife, whereupon he endeavored to do the same, but it caught somehow in his pocket, preventing him from pulling out the instrument. Then he ran, Mitchell after him. Sampson entered the Occidental saloon, followed by Mitchell, and the difficulty renewed. Mitchell was severely stabbed with a double-edged paper knife, sharp as a razor. Sampson was taken to the police station and released on a bond of $150 for disturbing the peace.

The wounded Mitchell walked to his room just back of Swindell's Printing House. He was bleeding terribly, and doctors Richard Swearingen and Frank McLaughlin were sent for. They did all they could for him, and when a *Statesman* reporter called shortly after midnight, he was resting quietly. The blade had entered at the point of the left shoulder, and the axillary artery was probably severed, the doctors thought, from the great flow of blood.

Damos, to his credit, made no such protests; perhaps age was mellowing the old man.

The professor informed a *Statesman* reporter one night during the Advent season of 1885 that he was tired of it all and that, if he could raise the money, he would purchase the property on Pecan Street, opposite the post office, and erect a five-story building. As a starter, he asked the reporter for five dollars but said "one dime" would answer, as it was late at night, with the banks closed.

Everyone agreed that time and the wintry blasts were dealing hard with the old man and demanded that the local authorities scour Damos and rig him out in clean clothes or contract with someone to have him fumigated. He smelled to heaven and was a positive nuisance.

Early in February 1886, Judge Zachary Fulmore had Damos hauled up before him and adjudged him insane. On the night before his appearance before Judge Fulmore, cold as it was, the professor had slept in the open hallway of the Hancock building with no covering but his bundle of papers.

Prior to his introduction into the courtroom, however, the services of "Big" Jim Alexander, considered the strongest man in Austin and one of the city scavengers, were secured, and he disrobed Damos, something that possibly had not occurred for a year or more, and gave him a good scouring off, after which a new suit of clothes was put on, his hair cut and the old man made to look quite respectable. Damos was sent to the asylum the next morning, arrangements having been made for his reception. Folks considered it an act of humanity.

The first attempt to place him in the asylum was in May 1880. Charles Schaeffer was placed in the asylum one day that month, and later that evening, Damos was on the street and informed those he met that he had just returned from the asylum, where he had assisted in placing Schaeffer safely within the walls.

Damos was carried before Judge Smith and, after being examined by medical experts, was adjudged a lunatic and was ordered to be sent to the asylum. The professor was cleaned up, and just before starting for the asylum, he asked the judge for paper and a pen, which were furnished to him. He sat down to a table in the courtroom and wrote, in a neat and legible hand, a note addressed to a Mr. Peacock, an attaché of the *Statesman* office:

> *Mr. Peacock, ask the cashier to write down for a subscription the* Democratic Statesman *for one year.*
>
> *A.E. Damos.*

But the asylum refused to take him, and he was brought back to the city to resume his interminable peregrinations.

In July 1882, Officer Oberwetter took Damos in charge and placed him in the city jail. The old man had gotten his clothes torn and was in a horrible plight. The county judge was requested to supply relief but stated that he was unable to do anything. But something had to be done. His condition was a standing disgrace, and the dictates of common humanity, if nothing else, suggested some action on his behalf.

Damos was turned over to the county authorities on a charge of lunacy. He was thoroughly washed and cleaned, furnished with a new suit of clothes and confined in jail. After being supplied with the new suit of clothing, he was turned out of jail the next morning. Damos was drunk as a lord before nightfall.

Just weeks later, after his permanent commitment to the asylum in 1886, the people of Austin were already missing him on the streets and wondering how he was doing.

After a month at the asylum, he was pronounced as getting along well, but he did miss his bundle of papers and his usual drinks of stale beer.

He died in the asylum on March 5, 1887, and the *Statesman*'s obituary read, in part, "The harmless old man, with the batch of newspapers on his bosom—a part of his hallucination—was, for long years, a familiar sight for the people of Austin." He was buried on the asylum grounds, and to this day, Austin State Hospital authorities refuse to release any information about him and the location of his grave unless the request comes from a family member.

THE SERVANT GIRL ANNIHILATORS

Town is fearfully dull, except for the frequent raids of the Servant Girl Annihilators, who make things lively during the dead hours of the night. If it were not for them, items of interest would be very scarce.
—William S. Porter (O. Henry) in a letter to a friend, May 1885

The "Annihilators" and their victims brought Austin into the worldwide spotlight for the first time.

I am not the end-all expert on what are commonly called the "servant girl murders." My interest in them is part of my larger interest in the style and quality of life in Austin, especially its low life and the mixing of the races, from the end of the Civil War to the turn of the century.

This was Austin's most violent era, and the servant girl murders served as sort of a catharsis. When this reign of terror ended on Christmas Eve 1885, life in Austin began to calm down, to the point that Will Porter wrote in 1894, "Bad men are out of date in Austin."

Several books have been written about the murders, and there are probably a dozen websites, at least two TV shows and one guided tour. We all have one thing in common: none of us has figured out who committed the murders. We do not know whether the murders were committed by a single fiend or an organized band, his or their race or whether the same fiend or fiends were responsible for all the attacks and murders. The murders will never be solved, and that is part of their enduring lurid charm. Unlike the Jack the Ripper murders, to which our servant girl murders are often compared, no postmortem photos

O. Henry. *Public domain.*

or detailed autopsies exist. The London victims were generally notorious prostitutes surgically killed in disreputable parts of London; the Austin victims were simple servants crudely mauled in largely respectable residential neighborhoods. The two killing sprees share almost nothing in common.

In all, only four Austin servant girls were murdered, all of them young women of color. A boyfriend and daughter were killed in two of the servant girl murders. The violent deaths of two white women who were not servants, but whose murders resembled those of the servant girls, are commonly included in the unlucky group of victims.

The servant girl murders were but part of a much larger succession of dozens of violent (but not fatal) attacks on servant girls, black and white, that occurred during 1885.

These attacks and murders did not occur in a vacuum. They reflected a larger phenomenon that had existed in Austin for the previous ten years, a perception that Austin was headed down the road to hell, such that in 1880, it elected Ben Thompson, one of the most notorious pistoleros of his era, to the office of city marshal.

Ben put a bite in crime in Austin until July 1882, when he went down to San Antonio and killed a gambling hall owner with whom he had issues. After he was acquitted in 1883 and came back to Austin a private citizen, he became a one-man shooting spree until he journeyed back down to San Antonio in March 1884 and was ambushed and shot dead by his previous victim's partner.

Nine months after Thompson's death, the first of the servant girl murders began. Not that there was any connection between the two, but the general feeling was that Austin's police force had been incapable of keeping a lid on crime in Austin since Thompson's departure from office.

Gonzales County Jail cell, 1887. *Photo by Samantha Zelade.*

The spree began with the murder of Mollie Smith, a young mulatto cook, on the frigid night of December 30, 1884. She was bludgeoned to death in her room—her face smashed to a pulp—and then dragged into the backyard near the outhouse, where she was left, nearly nude. There were indications she had been raped. Her boyfriend, Walter Spencer, had been badly beaten about the head as well but survived. Mollie, like all the victims of color, was buried in an unmarked grave in what was called the "colored burying ground."

William Brooks, a former lover of Mollie's, was arrested and kept a few weeks in jail before being released for lack of evidence.

To better understand this year of terror, it's essential to examine attacks that did not result in murder because the survivors gave details of the attacks that the deceased obviously could not reveal.

By March 14, 1885, Austin felt itself it gripped by terror, as the *Austin Statesman* commented:

> *Not less than four outrageous acts occurred in this city before the break of day yesterday. It is getting to be monotonous work, this perpetual narration of midnight marauders and their diabolical deeds.*
>
> *Some time after midnight a colored woman employed as a cook at the residence of Dr. W.A. Morris was aroused by a violent shaking at the door of her apartment. She screamed. Her husband seized his pistol and fired twice at the parties outside who then retreated to the street and threw a number of rocks violently against the door and side of the room. The terrified woman kept screaming until a number of neighbors were aroused, and the villains beat a retreat. It was impossible to follow them up in the darkness.*
>
> *Two colored servant girls, sleeping in the rear of Major Joe Stewart's house, were frightened out of their wits by repeated knocks at the door, coupled with demands of entrance. They refused to open the door, whereupon the intruder tried to open the window. The terrified girls then bolted out of the room. The fellow ran after them, caught one of them and threw her to the ground. Her screams brought several to her rescue speedily, but the villain escaped.*
>
> *The third outrage occurred at the residence of Mrs. Parrish on West Pecan street. The room in which a colored woman was sleeping was entered and she was treated to the most brutal treatment. She said both her assailants were negroes, one of them a yellow man painted black. She identified one of them as a mulatto barber who was promptly arrested.*

In the fourth incident, the fellow was foiled and ran off.

If the above state of things keeps up, the *Statesman* wrote, "Austin will stand in need of vigilantes to rid the city of the roughs that thus go about and commit every species of felony with seeming impunity. No house seems safe from their raids and every citizen should keep a bright look out and well loaded shotgun in handy proximity to his bedside."

On the night of March 19, after a week when scarcely a night passed without some unprotected female domestic being the victim of attempted brutal assaults, two Swedish servant girls were attacked in their apartment near the university.

The girls were aroused just before 1:00 a.m. by a knocking at the door. One of them arose, lit the lamp and was standing in the middle of the room holding it when a shot fired through the window on the opposite side and grazed her neck. She flew screaming from the apartment to the outdoors, where one of the ruffians seized her and started, unsuccessfully, to drag her away. Her repeated shrieks aroused her employer's family, several of whom came to the rescue, but they saw no assailant, and all thought the attack was ended. In the meantime, the other girl, Christine, had gone into the kitchen and was talking with Mrs. John Pope when a second shot was fired through a broken pane of glass, striking the poor girl about midway between the shoulder blade and spinal column, inflicting a dangerous wound.

Several hours later, a black girl who worked as a cook for Miss Ella Rust on East College Avenue was similarly visited. It wasn't the first time, and the girl was on the lookout for an assault. The fellow first broke out several panes of glass and then tore loose a wire screen across the window, demanding all the time to be let in. Grabbing a pistol, the girl blazed away at the man. Alas, it was a self-cocking weapon that she did not know how to manage, and she was unable to repeat the shot. The villain then coolly walked to the door and tried to push it open. The girl's cries brought a family member on the scene. Standing in plain view of the intruder, she ordered him to leave. His reply was to hurl a rock at her, followed by another and another. She then gave a general alarm, and two neighbor men, pistols in hand, sailed out but were too late to put a bullet where it would do the most good.

In both the foregoing cases, the parties attacked stated that their assailants were black men.

Several other houses were visited the same night, among them county attorney Frank Morris's home. None of the attacks was successful, but they were additional proof of the terrible state of existing affairs.

Night after night, outrages became more and more appalling. Outrages had been growing in number every succeeding night until terror reigned among the females of every household. Fear seized them as the twilight came and didn't leave them even in dreams until daylight came, when sneak thieves and assassins hid away and rested before their next nightly prowl of rape and murder. Dozens of outrages, the *Statesman* said, had been attempted on unprotected women since Mollie Smith's murder.

Early in the morning of April 29, after several weeks of relative calm, a black "ruffian" entered the sleeping apartment of Mrs. Edward Benkhe. She woke up and sprang from her bed, but the "scoundrel" seized her and threw her to the floor. The ensuing struggle did not wake her husband, who was in an adjoining room. The assailant covered her mouth with his huge hands to stifle her screams. She fought back, taking a knife from his hands, with which he threatened to kill her. Had not Mrs. Benkhe been possessed of great strength, she would doubtless have been a victim of this fiend's brutal passion.

About one o'clock that same morning, Mrs. John Calloway's colored cook underwent a similar experience. She was alone in her room in the rear of the house. Some dresses hung on a line in the yard. Her assailant put on one of these and entered her apartment. When she woke up, he was clutching her throat. Drawing out a razor, he threatened to kill her if she screamed. Just at this time, two other colored women came in the yard and, seeing the open door, called to the woman inside. This scared the fellow, who rushed out past the women, making vicious cuts at them with his razor as he went by. His strange appearance caused them to cry out, and the noise awoke Orlando Caldwell, who lived next door. He snatched up a pistol, ran out into the yard and saw a black man trying to divest himself of a woman's dress, cutting off the sleeves with the razor. Caldwell aimed but missed. He had forgotten to load the gun. The rascal leaped over a fence into an alley and disappeared. The mutilated garment was found the next morning with bloodstains on it, suggesting that its wearer had cut himself in his attempt to disrobe.

On May 7, thirty-year-old Eliza Shelley was murdered in her cabin. She had been a cook for a family named Johnson for about six weeks. In the dawn hours, her employer heard a child's screams coming from the cabin and sent her niece to investigate. Eliza's wounds included a hole above one ear and another between the eyes, probably from an ice pick. She had also been hit with an axe above the right eye, down into the brain. As was characteristic in the previous deaths, the room was in great disorder. Eliza had been dragged from her bed and placed atop a mound of quilts and blankets in a position that hinted at rape. No weapons were found, and only one footprint, outside in sandy soil, was found.

Her three young sons, who slept in bed with her, offered no information, except the oldest boy, who said a man entered the room and that he awoke while his mother and other brothers still slept. The man seized him and told the boy to keep quiet or he would kill him. He could not tell whether the man was black or white. The man pulled the boy into a corner, made him lie down and covered him with a blanket. He went back to sleep and knew nothing of what happened to his mother until he awoke at dawn.

The *Statesman* called on the governor to offer a reward for the murderer's arrest, stating that it did not matter that the victim was an obscure colored woman. Her life was as dear to her, and should be held as sacred, as that of the proudest lady in the land.

A man who had lived with Eliza briefly was arrested on circumstantial evidence. There was nothing positive against him, though many believed him guilty.

Eliza's murder was followed in short order, on May 23, by that of Irene Cross, who lived near Scholz Garden. She was sleeping in her room but had left the door unlocked for her son, who kept late hours. The fiend came in. The startled woman cried out. He assaulted her with a long sharp knife, perhaps a razor, and cut a horrible gash in her arm, severing an artery. Another frightful wound was inflicted on her head, very nearly scalping her. She died a few hours later, around sunrise. A jury of inquest found the usual verdict of death at the hands of an unknown person.

Her death was third on the list of women of color who had been mysteriously murdered in just under six months.

Anyone who has spent a summer in Austin knows how unbearable life can be, even with the air conditioner running 24/7. Back in 1885, you were lucky to find a ceiling fan to sit under and be rich enough to order a drink with ice. For whatever reason, the servant girl murderer(s) took the summer off. Crime went on as usual: burglaries, assaults, public drunkenness, minor shootings, even an infanticide, but no sensational murders or servant girl assaults.

On Sunday morning, August 30, between four and five o'clock, some brute entered the kitchen of Valentine Weed, on East Cedar Street, where Rebecca Ramey and her eleven-year-old daughter, Mary, were sleeping. He sandbagged Rebecca and wounded her in the left temple with some sharp instrument and then dragged Mary into the wash house adjoining, ravished her and then drove an iron pin into both her ears, killing her.

Becky said that she didn't recognize the person who committed the awful deed, that she was asleep when the attack was made and didn't know what had happened until the doctors came to examine her wounds.

Several local ne'er-do-wells were pulled in for examination, but there was no solid evidence to connect them to the crime.

A local citizen, writing in the *Statesman*, called for a drastic overhaul of the police force:

> *Another terrible crime, the seventh in a series of similar ones within the past year, has been committed. It was made known about five o'clock Sunday morning, by Mr. Weed, and the news of the horrible tragedy spread rapidly.*

Everybody was talking of the bloody deed, but the city marshal did not reach the scene until after 11 o'clock, nearly seven hours after the startling information had been sent out by Mr. Weed.

The inefficiency of the police management of the city for the past year or two, has been apparent to the occasional observer. The ineffectual attempts to ferret out those who have committed the horrible, mysterious murders in this city in the recent past enforces this assertion. All the surroundings connected with these murders indicate that they have been cunningly planned, carefully directed and intelligently consummated. No ignorant negro, such as is now under arrest, committed the crimes. They were conceived, and especially the one of Sunday, with a superior intelligence, and brain work of a higher order will have to be invoked to discover the perpetrators. The crime of Sunday can hardly be laid at the door of an ignorant negro. History of outrages upon women by negroes proves this. They rarely ever deliberately murder their victims, and experience shows that nine times out of ten they invariably leave some clue which leads to their identification and arrest.

Early in the morning of September 29, a report flashed over the city that another murderous assault had been committed on several colored servants—twenty-two-year-old Grace Vance and twenty-one-year-old Orange Washington—in a small wooden shanty on San Marcos Street. Washington, Grace's common-law husband, was found lying across the bed, almost dead, with ghastly wounds in his head while another woman, Patsy Gibson, was observed reclining on her left elbow on a pallet on the floor, badly wounded, conscious but incognizant. Patsy, a cook at a neighboring residence, was spending the night at Grace's. At this juncture, it was noted that Grace was missing. There was blood on the shanty's western window, and farther up in the same direction, blood was seen on the fence. After following a bloody trail some seventy-five yards from her room, the murdered Grace was found, just back of a neighbor's stable, weltering in pools of blood, her head almost beaten into a jelly. Lucinda Boddy, another guest of the murdered couple, was the only one who seemed to recognize the assaulting party. He had struck her, and she got up, lit a lamp and spoke to him, saying, "Oh, Dock, don't do it!"

His reply was, "God damn you, don't you look at me." Looking around the room, Lucinda saw what had been done, viewed the bloody scene and again said, "Oh, Dock, don't do it." He again replied, "God damn you, don't look at me. Blow out that light." Lucinda jumped out of the window and rushed toward Major William Dunham, who, by this time, had come out of his house armed with a gun. The girl threw her arms around Dunham, saying, "We are all killed and Dock Woods did it."

Dock Woods, another notorious local criminal, was arrested but was soon let loose after he proved his innocence.

White Austinites had many theories that summer about the servant girl assaults and murders. Was a secret organization trying to stamp out "negro prostitution" and compel the race, if they lived together, to live in the bonds of matrimony? Women left alive to describe the circumstances of the attacks said several times that they identified the man but shortly afterward denied that they did. Had they had been instructed by some secret power that held them under terror? Were the murders being perpetrated by a band of black men out of a spirit of pure cussedness and reckless wickedness?

Austin was considered the best-armed city in the country at the time. The gunsmiths did a wholesale business, and the *Statesman* declared that each home in town probably contained at least fourteen rounds of ammunition.

By mid-October, a police officer told a *Statesman* reporter,

it is next to impossible to see an Austin negro woman upon the streets, and this assertion is not confined to the women alone, most of the streets of the city are as lonesome, after dark, as a country graveyard. Men are about as scarce upon the streets as women. I have been to several negro's [sic] houses of late, and have yet to find a house where the negroes do not sleep with hatchets, pistols and all kinds of deadly weapons under their pillows. There is a reign of terror among the entire negro population, and many of them are so badly frightened that they tremble when accosted and show many signs of being in abject terror of the visits of the midnight assassin. Others have become so badly frightened that they, like the Arabs of old, have folded their tents and silently stolen away.

How are the white people? Do they show signs of being terrorized?

A large percent of them appear to be badly frightened. It would amuse you to take a peep at the gunsmith shops. The smiths have got more than they can do for weeks to come. People call every day to have their "pops" put in repair. Some of the weapons look as if they had served in the revolutionary war, while some of the pistols are so small they would be lost in a vest pocket. Regular curiosities, fished up from old barrels and gutters to do service. While a large percent of these customers are negroes you can find a right peart sprinkling of whites.

The year of butchery came to a close on Christmas Eve 1885, with the murders of two white women who, while not servant girls, and vastly different in age and lifestyle, were killed in similar, ghastly manners.

About eleven o'clock that night, forty-four-year-old Susan Hancock, the wife of M.H. Hancock, a mechanic, was attacked with an axe. She did not die immediately. A *Statesman* reporter found doctors dressing her ghastly wounds. Her skull was fractured in two places, and blood was coming from both ears. Her groans of agony were piercing, and with what seemed to be her expiring breath, cupfuls of blood were emitted from her mouth.

Hancock said that his daughter had gone out to a Christmas Eve party somewhere in the neighborhood, and as she was not expected to be out late, the doors were left unlocked.

Something woke him up, and he suddenly realized that his house had been robbed. Feeling for his clothes, he discovered that his pants were gone. Getting up, he went to his wife's room, which was lighted by the full glare of the moon, and he was almost paralyzed by the sight of clots of blood on the bed; his wife was nowhere to be seen. He went out a back door, and at the back of his yard, he saw his wife, lying on the ground, weltering in a pool of blood.

Picking her up, he started back to the house, all the time calling his neighbor for help.

The neighbor helped Hancock carry his butchered wife into the parlor, and in a few minutes, the doctors arrived.

City marshal James Lucy immediately set about trailing the murderous villain(s). The city's bloodhounds were brought to the house and given a start in the direction in which Hancock said he saw two men jump the fence.

The dogs worked all right for a short while, but the officer who handled them brought them back and gave them another start, taking a trail in a westerly direction, or up the river.

While still gathering notes, kneeling by the side of the dying lady, a shrill voice from the street cried that another murder had been committed in the second ward, on the premises of James Phillips, a well-known architect and builder. Phillips's son, James Phillips Jr., and his wife, eighteen-year-old Eula Phillips, occupied a small room in the house. Jimmy was a drunkard, and Eula was a sexual libertine who had cuckolded Jimmy on a number of occasions during their brief marriage and had at least one herbally induced abortion.

Eula used what were known then as houses of assignation for her trysts, where rooms could be rented by the hour or night. On several occasions, Eula had received several of her lovers at the house of Fanny Whipple, a notorious woman of color, with the full knowledge of her mother- and sister-in-law.

That night, Jimmy and Eula and their little boy retired to bed as usual. Sometime past midnight, the household was awakened by yells from Jimmy calling for someone. The door of the room was found open.

The pillows and bedclothes presented a horrid spectacle, saturated with blood and reddened with gore. Jimmy Phillips lay on his right side, with a deep wound just above the ear made with an axe that lay beside the bed. Eula was not there, but their child remained, besmeared with blood but unharmed. A trail of blood, still fresh on the floor, was immediately followed out into the yard, and a few feet from the fence, at the door of the water closet, Eula was found dead.

Her body was entirely nude, and a piece of timber was laid across her breasts and arms, evidently used for the most hellish and damnable purpose. Her hands were outstretched, and a great pool of blood, still warm and scarcely coagulated, stood in a little trench, into which the life current had flowed down from the unfortunate victim.

Eula's body had been dragged from the room, but whether Eula was killed in the room or was awakened by the assault on her husband and attempted to escape could not be determined. It was believed, however, that the assassins stifled her voice and that she was still alive when dragged into the yard, where she was outraged and the last and fatal blow delivered.

The body's position indicated that a second party had assisted in perpetuating the devilish act, as both hands were held down by pieces of wood, in which position the fiends left their victim and in which she must have died.

The elder Phillips stated that while this most horrible crime was being committed, everything was as silent as usual. No cutting seems to have been heard, so skillfully did the inhuman butcher or butchers carry out a crime worthy of the imps of hell.

When asked if he knew who struck him, Jimmy groaned deeply and said he did not.

On December 29, the last attack of the yearlong spree occurred. At a late hour, an officer heard screams for help from a cottage on Waller Creek. A woman and little girl, half dead with fright, explained that they had seen a man in one of the windows and that another had gained entrance to the building and bedroom and had attempted to chloroform them. Both men, they said, had run off when the alarm was first raised, but not before the woman got a good look at them. She said both were white and well dressed, and pointing out the direction they took, the officer got on their trail and followed them down Waller Creek, where he lost sight of them. He learned subsequently that they had followed the creek to Pecan Street, where they were seen to climb up the bank and hastily proceed in the direction of Congress Avenue, where all trail of them was lost.

Rewards were posted in January for the arrest and conviction of the party or parties responsible for each of the victims. Naturally, the two white women got first priority, at $1,000 each, but a reward of $1,000 was also offered for the arrest and conviction of the perpetrator or perpetrators first convicted of any one of the colored victims.

At the time, of course, no one knew that the murderous spree had ended. On January 14, the *Statesman* noted, as the full moon approached:

> *One thing is certain: all the terrible and cruel assassinations which occurred in this city during last year, with but one exception, were committed in the light of the moon, and below will be found the time which elapsed after the full moon when the horrible crimes were perpetrated.*
>
> *The first victim to fall in the series of bloody mysteries was Mollie Smith, on the night of December 30th, 1884, and the night of the full moon.*
>
> *Just four months and seven days after, or on May 7th, or exactly seven days after the full of the moon, Eliza Shelley was hacked to pieces.*
>
> *On May 23rd, nine days after the new moon and 16 days after Eliza Shelley met her death, Irene Cross was assassinated.*
>
> *About three months after, and five days past full moon, on August 30th, the insatiable fiend cruelly murdered and out raged little Mary Ramey.*
>
> *On September 28th, nearly one month after Mary's death, Gracy Vance and Orange Washington were killed, just four days after the full of the moon.*
>
> *On December 24th, Mrs. Phillips and Mrs. Hancock met their horrible fate, and it was exactly three days past the full of the moon.*
>
> *The moon will soon be full again, and then will wane. Will it be on a scene of blood and cruel and ghastly death?*

It must be pointed out that Austin's nighttime lighting was wretchedly inadequate, consisting of weakly lit gas streetlamps located mostly along Congress Avenue. They were turned off during the nights of the full moon, since the moon gave off more light than they did. It was considered brazenly odd that the murders were not committed in the darkness of the new moon, and folks wondered if there wasn't something about the light of the moon that brought out the maniac in an otherwise normal person.

Several of today's armchair sleuths have blamed at least one of the murders on Alex Mack, a local troublemaker (who also happened to be black), based on a bloody footprint found in the snow. Mack's foot was the same size and missing the same toe. Compelling? The police didn't think so, even if he was a thorn in their side. He died of a gunshot wound less than a year later, during which time no further murders of the type were committed. Was it Alex Mack? Your guess is as good as anybody's.

Only one person was ever brought to trial: Jimmy Phillips, for the murder of Eula. He was convicted, but the case was appealed and a new trial ordered, which ended in a mistrial. Phillips was set free. Eula is buried in an unmarked grave in the Phillips family plot somewhere up on the Oakwood Cemetery hill. Susan Hancock is buried in lot 459, the only victim whose exact resting place is known.

Rumors continued for years thereafter, and common wisdom was that the murders would eventually be solved, most likely by someone's deathbed confession. With the advent of Jack the Ripper a few years later, there was speculation that Austin's servant girl murderer had moved to London to ply his trade. It was pointed out that the advent of fast trains and steamships had made it very easy for serial killers to move about the world, killing at whim.

In February 1889, a series of foul murders in Managua, Nicaragua, were also thought to possibly be the work of the Austin murderer.

The most enduring theory as to the identity of the servant girl murderer centered around the "Malay Cook," who was also considered a suspect in London's Whitechapel murders.

The November 17, 1888 edition of the *Statesman* ran this intriguing story:

A Strange Coincident.
A Malay cook suspected in London.

A Malay cook suspected in Austin three years ago. A strange coincident [sic], *to say the least.*
During the year of the thrilling, startling and bloody tragedies, when dread and gloomy uneasiness brooded over the city, there was a Malay cook plying his avocation within her limits. The first and second and third and fourth, and all the murders up to little Mary Ramey, had occurred without his having been suspected. The night of little Mary's murder was clear, with the full moon riding high up in the heavens. It was about 4 o'clock when, her body still warm, members of the family where she lived, having been attracted by the groans of her mother, who had been seriously wounded, discovered her.

On that morning, so the story goes, precisely 30 minutes after the clock on the city hall pealed out the hour of two, a man apparently half seas over struggled up from the depths of the slums in the First ward. Seemingly, he was beastly drunk, and it was with difficulty and laborious exertion that he maintained his feet. Like a rudderless ship on a turbulent sea, he tossed about until he reached the neighborhood of the International depot, and drifted eastward until he reached the Avenue. Here he glided into smooth waters and settled down to steady, easy sailing. In truth, he mysteriously transformed himself, and from being drunk as a lord he became as sober as a priest.

So went the tale of one of the best detectives engaged in the work of unraveling the crime.

From where the new depot now stands this man steered a direct course up the Avenue to Sixth street down which he turned and hurried eastward to Trinity, thence southward to Pine, and then to where he committed the murder. He was traced to the spot, then all was lost. Who he was, no one knows.

Was he a Malay cook?

Certain it is that some three or four blocks from the scene of the tragedy it is said a Malay cook slept. He was rarely seen about town and nothing was known of his history. That he claimed to be a cook and was undoubtedly a Malay was about all there was known of him.

It turned out, however, that on the morning of the cruel murder of the little girl, he suddenly fell under a cloud of suspicion, and it was intensified by the discovery of fresh blood in a pool of water not far from his sleeping apartments. The murderer had stopped there to wash his hands. At least that was one of the many theories advanced at the time.

The Malay was shadowed for some time and then things went back into their normal condition and the city blissfully forgot all about the murders which had been flashed over the continent, bringing her prominently into view, and making her the tale of every hamlet and village in the land.

Then followed the Christmas eve crimes, with all their ghastly, shuddering details. Then it was that the attention of the detectives was again called to the Malay, and he was a suspect. He was kept under detectives' eyes, hoping that something definite would be found to warrant his arrest.

One morning, during an unguarded moment, he suddenly disappeared, and the Malay cook was lost sight of in the shuffle then going on, and was forgotten until attention was attracted by the cablegram alluded to at the outset saying a Malay cook is suspected of the London murders.

Three of the most bloody and cruel of the Austin murders occurred in the quarter of the city where this Malay is said to have slept, and none of them were over three or four blocks off. This, of itself, is somewhat singular. A Malay cook suspected in London; a Malay cook suspected in Austin.

Strange indeed.

Is the Whitechapel Malay cook and the Austin Malay cook one and the same?

It had been ascertained that a Malay cook calling himself Maurice had been employed at the Pearl house in 1885 and that he left sometime in January 1886.

So who was/were the murderer(s)? Your guess is as good as anyone's. The murders could have been individual crimes of passion of lover against lover, but that seems highly unlikely, given their frequency that year. Love-inspired tragedies usually happened only once or twice a year and involved shootings or other less grisly methods of killing. The perps were usually captured, or in some instances, they committed suicide afterward. The theory of an organized vigilance group seeking moral justice doesn't hold much water either. To me, the theory of the Malay cook makes as much sense as anything else, and that precious little. It is important to remember that the sciences of fingerprint identification and blood typing did not yet exist.

Stephen Saylor's novel, *A Twist at the End*, does a good job of putting the murders in the context of a larger Austin.

"SHOULD WE HAVE ANOTHER SUCH LEGISLATURE, WOULD IT NOT BE WELL TO DISSOLVE OUR STATE GOVERNMENT AND GET ATTACHED TO THE INDIAN TERRITORY?"

The lawmaking process is often compared to making sausage. Little good ever comes from any Texas legislative session, but some legislatures grind out particularly wretched sausage. The Nineteenth Legislature (1885) was possibly the rudest, most feckless and most violent legislature in Texas history.

Ah, where to begin with the carryings-on of the Nineteenth…

Let's start with the evening of Wednesday, March 11, when a disgraceful scene marred forever the history of legislation in Texas.

The Senate was discussing a bill abolishing the office of insurance commissioner, its supporters claiming that the commissioner was little more than a newspaper clipping collector and filer, and that any clerk could do the job. Augustus Houston of Bexar County made an elaborate and forcible argument in favor of its retention.

William Davis of Cooke County replied in his characteristic style and took occasion, as he often did, to ridicule. He compared Houston to a "strutting turkey gobbler."

At the conclusion of Davis's speech, Houston rose to a question of privilege and stated that in debates, criticisms were often indulged in, but never before had the personal appearance of any member been dragged into the fray until that "little yellow, sallow-faced mummy and blackguard from Cooke" saw fit to allude to him. He was ready to settle the matter outside the chamber or either within or outside the state, as the senator might select.

From On a Mexican Mustang Through Texas: From the Gulf to the Rio Grande, *by Sweet and Knox, Chatto and Windus, Piccadilly, 1884.*

Confusion followed, and the Senate president instructed the sergeant-at-arms to arrest the two senators. Comparative quiet was restored without this extreme measure, but intense excitement prevailed in the lobbies.

Davis arose and said that any senator who would take advantage of his position on the Senate floor to insult a member was a deliberate coward, poltroon and pusillanimous blackguard and that if he (Davis) wanted to raise a fight he would do it outside the Senate chamber.

As he said this, Houston passed from the Senate floor into the lobby, saying as he did so, "Come out, then."

Davis said he would not go out into a crowd, where he would be prevented from fighting, but that he could be found on the streets, at his boardinghouse or anywhere else outside the chamber.

After quiet was fully restored, Davis took the floor and stated that he had not intended to insult anyone in the heat of the debate and he was sorry that offense had been taken.

Houston replied that if that was the case, he felt sorry, too, and took back all that he had said.

That extraordinary scene in the Senate chamber was all the chief topic of discussion the next day. The belligerent senators had yet to encounter each other, and mutual friends were trying to preserve the peace. There was little hope of an actual reconciliation, but perhaps a difficulty might be staved off. There was no doubt that a very bad feeling prevailed and very little business would be done during the remainder of the session. The Senate was

A SPIRITED DEBATE IN THE TEXAS LEGISLATURE.

From On a Mexican Mustang Through Texas: From the Gulf to the Rio Grande, *by Sweet and Knox, Chatto and Windus, Piccadilly, 1884.*

hopelessly cut up into hostile factions, and bickering and antagonism would destroy the hope of the business of the public being cared for.

"Back in the day," journalists tended to protect the reputations of the sinners they covered—but only up to a point. By March 19, the *Galveston Daily News* had had enough of the Nineteenth's shenanigans and ripped the covers off of events in the Senate chamber on Monday night, March 9:

> *During the delivery of this speech the senate chamber was a perfect bedlam—shouting, gesticulating, remonstrating, denouncing from all corners of the chamber, pistols were passed around, as cards are dealt at a whist-table. Messengers were dispatched for pistols, knives were taken out and opened, and for a while everyone present was morally certain that bloodshed, if not slaughter, was imminent.*

The hostilities extended beyond the statehouse. A number of legislators were eating supper at Bulian's restaurant on the evening of March 19. Mr. Merriweather, of Frio County, came in and took a seat. He had a stick in his hand with which he kept tapping Dr. Camp, the member from Limestone. Camp at first paid no attention but finally objected. Merriweather had been drinking and was ripe for a row. Some emphatic words passed, and a fight was prevented only through the intervention of friends. The difficulty was, however, renewed on the sidewalk not long after, and flourishing their walking canes, both the gentlemen made at each other. Speaker Upton, in endeavoring to act as peacemaker, caught one of the blows, a sorry reward for his benevolent intentions. Then others again interfered, and the row was stopped for the night.

On March 28, the *Dallas Herald* ran the following:

Prepared for War

> *A few days since, when war was raging in the legislature, and the lie and "sich" was being hurled promiscuously by the members, the constituents of our representative, Mr. R.S. Kimbrough, purchased and expressed him a six-shooter, with the injunction to defend the honor and good name of Dallas county at all hazards. Yesterday the following reply, which explains itself, was received:*
> *Austin, March 27, 1885— W.G. Sterrett, J.G. Stephens, et al, Dallas, Texas:*
> *My Dear Friend: The "gun" came to hand O.K.—charge 25 cts. Many thanks for the same and accompanying kind expressions. I have loaded her*

*up and am waiting for an opportunity to "distinguish" myself. My friends
were very thoughtful, indeed, for a statesman working for $2 per day here
would never accumulate enough to buy a 50-cent pistol with which to defend
himself and country. I needed it, and my only regret is that you didn't think
of my poor, lone condition among savages sooner. Again tendering my most
heartfelt thanks to one and all, I am yours for war and reform.*

R.S. Kimbrough

P.S.—The senators don't come in the house now, except when I am out. K.

After these preliminary rounds, real blood finally began to flow.

That same morning, March 28, an *Austin Statesman* headline blared:
"Cutting to Kill."

Between ten and eleven o'clock on the evening of March 27, a very
serious stabbing affray occurred almost in front of the Avenue Hotel,
involving Tobias Mitchell, correspondent of the *St. Louis Globe-Democrat*, and
Alexander Sampson, calendar clerk of the Senate.

The origin of the row was a caricature of Sampson in the March 25
issue of the *Globe-Democrat*, one of a series of burlesque pictures of members
of the legislature, with some little accompanying description of the man.
Sampson was not at all pleased with his, only a rear view being presented,
and his ill temper was ill concealed. The sketch, though a burlesque on the
surface, along with the accompanying brief biographical narrative, conveyed
a deeper meaning in light of subsequent developments:

> *This presents a view of the handsomest part of Major Alex Sampson, the
> calendar clerk of the Senate. He is the only representative of the Israelites
> in that body, and has a great reputation for "being seen" as he terms it,
> or shaping the course of legislation for a reasonable consideration. He is a
> daisy at securing free railroad passes for himself and "particular friend,"
> or none at all. Like all of his race, he is possessed of the strong ability to
> look out for number one, and it is a cold day when a senator can get him to
> calendar a bill conveniently.*

Other men occupying far more honorable positions with quite as much
reputation at stake were hit equally as hard, both by pen and picture, and yet
did not consider themselves insulted.

Sampson claimed that he and Mitchell met on the sidewalk near the
Avenue Hotel. Sampson told Mitchell that he had been given a rough deal
in the paper and cursed the man who did it in terms not fit to be printed.

At this, he said Mitchell drew a knife, whereupon he endeavored to do the same, but it caught somehow in his pocket and he could not pull it out. Then he ran, Mitchell after him. Sampson entered the Occidental saloon, followed by Mitchell, and the difficulty was renewed. Mitchell was severely stabbed. Policeman Jim Williams came and arrested both men. Sampson was taken to the police station and released on a bond of $150 for disturbing the peace.

Mitchell walked to his room. He was bleeding terribly. Doctors Richard Swearingen (state health officer) and Frank McLaughlin were sent for, and they did all they could. The blade had entered at the point of the left shoulder and passed downward in the direction of the axillary artery. The artery was probably severed, the doctors thought, from the great flow of blood. They would not allow him to be talked to, for his life appeared in danger at the moment. (He recovered.)

A friend who heard it from the wounded man's lips told Mitchell's side of the story. It differed from Sampson's statement in one important particular. He admitted having gone into the saloon after Sampson, but his better judgment began to assert itself, and wishing to avoid a scene, he was turning to go when Sampson suddenly sprang forward and stabbed him.

Mitchell was well known in Texas journalism. He was managing editor of the *Houston Post* before its demise, a well-built, muscular man, weighing about 180 pounds, and possessing great nerve. He was around forty years of age and generally popular, having pleasant manners and a genial smile for every man he met. Scarcely a newspaperman in Texas was better liked.

Although arrested only for disturbing the peace, Sampson would find a far more serious charge to confront the next morning.

Sampson hailed from Galveston, where he was a ward politician. Little was known about him except that when the legislature assembled, he sought to be, and was elected, the Senate's calendar clerk. In the early days of the session, he was earning a reputation as an efficient officer, winning golden opinions from the senators and others who came in contact with him. But his true motives gradually began to reveal themselves.

For more than a month, the moral atmosphere of the capital had been rendering an unpleasant odor. The lobby was filled with whispers of questionable doings, and members of both houses swapped reports of questionable methods indulged in by attaches of the legislature: of bills being extracted from the committee rooms, defaced, altered and mutilated; that officers, mostly clerks, of both houses were professional lobbyists who levied blackmail on every party who appeared before the legislature interested in either the passage or defeat of a bill.

They levied tribute on all who would yield up a dollar. The advocates of certain new counties were bled freely. When the gambling bill was up, the gamblers were sucked dry. A telegraph lobby that appeared was rich game. The "sailors bill" (which would have prevented foreign sailors from working beyond their ship's tackle in Texas ports) was tackled when it was first introduced, but it didn't produce much.

The grand stand of the session was made on the bucket shop bill. A bucket shop was a private establishment where a customer could put up a specified margin on gold, cotton or other commodities to be delivered on an agreed-upon date in the future. We call it futures dealing. Here the boys expected to make the blood flow freely. They looked for big returns and luxurious expenditures, and some of the ring's members had planned a trip to New York, Hot Springs and other points when the bucket shop bill was called up.

When the House convened on the morning of March 28, Representative Lorenzo Fisher of Galveston exposed Sampson and company. About a month earlier, Sampson had written a letter to a well-known bucket shop proprietor in Galveston, stating that a pending bill, the bucket shop bill—which would prohibit speculation in grain and stock futures—could be suppressed if the bucket shop men would pay Joseph Tryon, clerk of the house's Judiciary Committee No. 2, $1,500. The bill was killed by placing on it a rider that would also prohibit dealing in futures in cotton and other public exchanges.

The reading of Sampson's letter on the House floor created a great sensation. Fisher, in a vigorous speech, exposed the doings of the band of clerical blackmailers, who, he said, had infested the legislative halls since the opening of the session.

Sampson was expelled that day.

Tryon was a young man from Houston, according to the *Galveston News*. He was a generous, impulsive fellow, reckless and thoughtless and could easily be made a tool of by designing men. In conversation with a *News* correspondent following Sampson's expulsion, Tryon admitted that others made a cat's-paw of him, though with loyalty worthy of a better cause, he refused to squeal.

Tryon was expelled on March 30, the day before the legislature adjourned.

They returned to their respective home turfs, evidently welcomed with open arms, because in September 1886, Tryon was a candidate for Harris County attorney and Alex Sampson for Galveston County judge, which the *Galveston News* regarded as a rebuke to the Nineteenth Legislature.

Sampson would play a prominent role in Galveston's legal circles and politics for years to come.

The postmortems on the Nineteenth began weeks before its adjournment, and they cut to the bone.

The *Fort Worth Gazette* declared on March 18:

> The legislature has been at work now since the 13th of January, and has nothing but a few local bills and several disgraceful scenes, to show to the people as the result of its labors. Hasn't Texas just a wee bit too much of "good fellowship" in its legislature? A "devilish good fellow" may be in place around the stove of a courthouse room or a "store"; but men who make laws should be "honorable" men in "word and deed." "Tom, Dick, and Harry" and the slap on the shoulder may do for the street, but dignity, self-respect, and a regard for personal, as well as public, rights, are expected of statesmen. There is too much of big-boyism, "kids," "mugwumps," etc., at Austin, and the solons have not been without a certain newspaper encouragement in converting the legislative halls of the state into the play-ground of a village school. Indeed, it is likely, from the aid and comfort they received from one newspaper, that "the kids" actually grew to believe that people in Texas had suspended all business and were standing on tiptoe to see what "the boys" would do next; whether they would thump another newspaper man, put a mansard roof on a judge, or curse and abuse each other. Texas is sick and tired of this "kid" business, in the legislature as well as in the university.

The *Austin Statesman* nailed the lid on the coffin on April 9:

> The Nineteenth Legislature had no intelligent executive suggestions, until at the last hour Comptroller Swain took the bull by the horns and showed the necessity for increased taxation for State expenses, as well as for a law forcing payment for the use of lands set aside for educational purposes. The two measures suggested by him led to the only two valuable enactments of the Nineteenth Legislature.
>
> The Legislature failed to pass the granite bill—even permitting the capitol to be built of granite. Such was legislation to the Nineteenth Legislature. When will we have such another; and should we have another such legislature, would it not be well to dissolve our state government and get attached to the Indian Territory?

It's appropriate to close the books on a joke of a legislature with a joke about it from *Texas Siftings*:

We do not know how much good or bad the legislature has thus far accomplished. They are still grinding away, but the grinding is like the turning of the crank on a peanut roaster. A countryman from Onion creek watched a man who was turning the handle on a peanut roaster steadily for half an hour and then he asked:

"When are you going to play a tune?"

He had taken the peanut roaster for a hand organ. The legislators are still turning the crank, but we are unable to determine just yet whether it is a hand organ for the amusement of the people or a peanut roaster for their own private profit.

"WHY DON'T YOU USE IT, NOW THAT YOU HAVE YOUR HAND ON IT?"

Husband-wife murder-suicides are so common these days as to often rate nothing more than a passing headline and paragraph's description, but such was not the case in October 1890, when *Statesman* headlines blared on the twenty-eighth:

> *A Terrible Deed.*
> *W. Dornwell Attempts to Murder His Mistress and Then Kills Himself.*
> *The House Surrounded by a Curious Throng Madly Clamoring for a Sight of the Dead Man.*
>
> *Another crime was added to the criminal record of Austin yesterday when William Dornwell, better known as "Buffalo Bill," attempted to kill his mistress, Maggie Nulle, "a well-known character about town," and then turned the smoking revolver on himself and blew out his brains.*

Dornwell, called "Buffalo Bill" by nearly everyone who knew him, was a well-known figure about Austin. He was born and raised near Giddings, Lee County. He served as a Texas Ranger for some years and became an Austin police officer in the early part of 1886. He remained there until late 1888 or early 1889, whereupon he opened an all-night chili and lunch stand on East Pecan near the Driskill Hotel.

From the National Police Gazette, *New York, 1883.*

Maggie was from Blanco County, her maiden name being Maggie James. Her parents were dead, but two brothers were still living in Blanco County. Some years earlier with her husband, A.G. Nulle, and his partner, she went over to Mexico, where they went into the mining business. A dispute arose over some trivial matter, and Nulle's partner killed him.

Panorama of Austin, Texas, 1910. The Driskill Hotel can be seen on the right-hand side. *Library of Congress Prints and Photographs Division.*

Maggie drifted back to Texas and finally to Austin, where she met Dornwell. He left his wife and four little children to shift for themselves and went to live with Maggie at the Emigrant Hotel, where the terrible deed was done.

The Emigrant, situated at the corner of East Avenue and Fifth Street, was occupied by a number of women who made a questionable living by taking male boarders.

Recorder's Court clerk Neill McCashin, at the city hall, got a telephone call at 1:45 p.m. stating that a row was in progress at the Emigrant, in which "Buffalo Bill" was taking a very prominent part. Officer Rufus Bell went to investigate but reported that Dornwell had left the house and come uptown and that everything was quiet.

Another message was received at police headquarters at 3:30 p.m. that a shooting had taken place at the same house, and the caller requested that an officer be sent down. Officer Orlando Gibson found Dornwell lying on the floor gasping for breath and Maggie on her bed with blood streaming from a hole in her right cheek.

A *Statesman* reporter reached the house at 3:45 p.m. and, pushing his way through a crowd clamoring for admission, made his way up the narrow steps leading to the hall. On the landing at the top, he met Dornwell's wife, who had been inside to see the work of her dying husband and was being led back to her home by friends. As she wrung her hands and sobbed, the hearts of all present were touched in a manner far beyond description.

The reporter made his way into the narrow hall into which two rooms opened. In the first one, which faced the street, Maggie lay on the bed, moaning, her clothes saturated with blood flowing from the bullet hole in her cheek. Her face was horribly burned by the powder. Dr. Everett Hamilton was by her side, and she kept calling, "Oh, Doctor, please put me to sleep, it hurts me so." Dr. John Lewright soon came in, and together they probed and found the ball, which they cut out from the back of the neck. The ball entered just below the right eye and shattered the jawbone and then ranged down and around the base of the brain, lodging near the surface about the middle of the neck. After it was extracted, she continued to ask the doctors to put her to sleep but soon fell off into a heavy sleep caused by the anesthetic administered during the probing.

In the second room, in which the shooting was done, the dying man lay on the floor with his head over the doorsill and projecting out into the hall, presenting a sickening spectacle that made strong men turn their heads away and leave the house. As he lay there on his back, blood and brains oozed from the bullet wound in the back of his head about two inches above the ear, forming a gory pool on the hall floor.

Dornwell fired the fatal shot about 3:20 p.m., but he continued to gasp periodically and it was not until 4:35 p.m. that a long drawn breath and an awful gurgling sound in the throat told that he was a dead man.

The room in which the shots were fired was a little box, eight by ten feet, and in it were the cooking stove and table on which the noonday meal was spread.

Witness Dora Elders said:

> I was in the room at the Emigrant Hotel talking with Maggie Nulle. Mr. Jess Wilson was also in the room. About 3:00 p.m., the deceased came into the room and requested Maggie to go into another room with him and said he wanted to talk to her. She refused, saying to him, "You said that you intended to beat me and I will not go with you. I have no protection here." He said, "I will tell you what I have to tell you when we get into the room, and I will never bother you again after to-day." She again refused to go into the room. He then asked, "Then you will not go?" Then he said to her, "Where is the ring I gave you?" She replied, "I have it." He said, "You are a goddamned liar. Mr. Aaron Jones has got it," and immediately he put his hand on his hip pocket. When he put his hand on his back pocket Maggie said to him, "Why don't you use it, now that you have your hand on it?" He at once drew his pistol and pointed it at Maggie, gritting his teeth at the same time, and immediately he fired the shot, which struck Maggie in the face, and then he turned and looked a moment at Mr. Jess Wilson and then raised the pistol to his own head and fired two shots; at the first shot at his head he staggered back toward the door and after the second shot he fell with his head in the doorway leading to the hall. On Sunday, October 26, the day before the shooting, the deceased and Maggie Nulle quarreled all day, and he locked the door on her and threw the key out of the window.

Despite her terrible wound, Maggie survived.

By February 4, 1891, Maggie was up and out. She had been under the care of Dr. Hamilton and was at death's door for several months, but careful nursing and skillful medical attention brought her around all right.

But on the morning of July 27, 1891, Maggie was found lying on her bed, unconscious and evidently under the influence of a powerful narcotic.

For some time past, she had been living in a room over A.H. Achilles's store on the corner of Pecan and Colorado Streets and for several days had been despondent and out of spirits. Her friends did not think that she contemplated suicide; hence, no watch was kept over her.

The previous afternoon, Maggie wrote a note to an old and well-known citizen requesting him to call at her room the next morning. He did so but found the door locked, and no amount of banging and rattling would arouse the inmate.

Satisfied that something was wrong, the gentleman left and notified Officer John Kennerly. The two returned to the room and, gaining admission through a side door, found Maggie. They quickly called Dr. Hamilton, who applied an electric battery and resorted to other methods usual in such cases, but to no avail. Maggie died at about nine o'clock.

She left a note stating her name and date of birth; the name of her husband, A.G. Nulle, and the date of his death in 1886; and the names and dates of birth of her two children, Calvin and Edgar, who were living with an uncle near Crockett, Texas. She requested that her effects be sold to pay her debts and that her finger rings and a picture of "Buffalo Bill" be buried with her.

She had been living in Austin about four years. Before Dornwell shot her, she had an attractive face and was a prepossessing woman. Since her recovery, she had been taking in sewing. Her room, while poorly furnished, was neat and clean, and there were evidences that she was a woman of refined taste. Only thirty years old, she was buried by the city in lot 594.

LOVE LIES BLEEDING IN THEIR ARMS

Ten o'clock in the morning on June 30, 1903. Just another summer day in Austin, with the morning coolness surrendering to the heat of the day. State comptroller Robert Love was sitting at his desk in his capitol office discussing a religious question with the Reverend M.F. Cowden of Bonham (Love was a prominent worker in the Presbyterian Church and a steward in Presbyterian-affiliated Trinity University at Waxahachie).

Love had been writing letters that morning to twenty-seven lucky winners of scholarships to the various state "normals" (teacher training schools). He had made his choices from a list of over seventy-five applicants.

A few minutes after ten o'clock, W.G. Hill, who had previously worked in the comptroller's office for ten years, walked into Love's office. Love greeted him cordially, and the two shook hands. Love introduced Cowden to Hill, and then Hill drew a letter from his pocket, handed it to Love and requested that he read it.

Cowden, thinking it was a private matter, walked out of the office and was barely outside the door when he heard a shot, followed almost immediately by another.

No sooner had Love started reading the letter than Hill sprang to his feet, pulled out a pistol and fired two shots into Love's body, one above the heart, the other below. It was 10:20 a.m.

Love screamed, dropped the letter and fell backward from his chair.

Mission accomplished, Hill made for the door, where Clerk J.W. Stevens, Love's chief bookkeeper, who worked in an adjacent office, intercepted him. Cowden rushed back into the room and saw Stevens struggling with

Capitol hallway leading to the comptroller's offices. *Jack E. Boucher, 1966, Library of Congress Prints and Photographs Division.*

Hill. They scuffled through the first receiving clerk's office and out into the main hall, and while there, Hill attempted to pull his pistol around behind and shoot Stevens. Stevens held on to his shoulders and arms, and as they grappled, Hill's pistol discharged, the bullet entering Hill's abdomen. He fell a dead weight in Stevens's arms and was lowered gently to the floor, where he lay until taken to the hospital where he died at three o'clock. Love died one hour after the shooting, in his office, surrounded by his family.

A few minutes after the tragedy, the statehouse was packed with people eager to learn the details of the shooting. Governor S.W.T. Lanham was among the first on the scene, and Comptroller Love asked the governor to appoint Stevens to his position and that all of his clerks keep their positions. Lanham did not promise but said, "Don't you worry; I will take care of your official family."

As he was dying, Love managed to give a final statement: "Mr. Hill shot me. He presented a letter of endorsement to me for a place in the department. I was reading the letter when he shot me. I had asked him about his brother's wife's death. I regretted her death very much. Mrs. Hill was a good woman. I have no idea why he shot me. May the Lord bless him and forgive him. I cannot say more."

He lost consciousness at 11:15 a.m. and expired at 11:30 a.m.

Hill's letter was dyed in blood when picked up and read:

Governor S.W.T. Lanham. *Public domain.*

> *Dear Sir: Public office is a public trust. Public officers are created for the service of the people, and not for the aggrandizement of a few individuals. The practice of bartering department clerkships for private gain is a disgrace to the public service, and in this nefarious practice you are a "record breaker." You have robbed the state employees, and your incompetent administration has prompted others to rob the state.*
>
> *The man who, claiming to be a Christian, deprives others of employment without cause, is a base hypocrite and a tyrant.*
>
> *The greatest mind that ever gave its wisdom in the world, the mind of all others most capable of "umpiring the mutiny between right and wrong," said, "You take my life when you do take from me the means by which I live."*
>
> *If that be true, you are a murderer of the deepest crime or hue.*
>
> *Although I cannot help myself before laying life's burden down I shall strike a blow—feeble though it be—for the good of my deserving fellow man.*
>
> *"For the right, against the wrong.*
> *For the weak, against the strong."*
> *Yours truly, W.G. HILL.*

Love had discharged Hill from his position about a year earlier.

Hill was considered to be quiet and gentlemanly and was never known to drink or have any bad habits. At the time of the shooting, he held a good job in the office of the Austin water and light plant, so dire want could not have instigated the frenzy that prompted the shooting. The common opinion was that he had gone insane.

In spite of intense suffering, Hill managed to state that he had shot Love but not himself, as some had thought. "I shot Love because he did not treat me right. I want it understood that I did not shoot myself."

While Hill was still lying in the corridor, a bottle of laudanum was taken from his pocket, and reaching for it, he said, "Let me take that and die easy,"

"Democrats Ousting Radicals from Office." *From* Leslie's Weekly.

which led many to believe that he contemplated suicide after shooting Love. Both men left families.

The governor ordered all departments closed and the flag to be flown at half-mast. A few days later, he appointed Stevens as Love's successor.

Born in Franklin, Texas, in 1847, Robert Love grew up in Tehuacana in Limestone County and served in the Confederate army. After the war, he returned home and successfully farmed and raised livestock. In 1870, he married Lucy Townes Morgan. They had ten children.

Love began his political career as deputy sheriff of Limestone County in 1872. Love and his brother John were among the armed men who helped end Reconstruction in Texas, standing at the capitol stairs to protect the members of the newly elected, Democrat-dominated legislature gathered on the capitol's second floor from Governor Edmund J. Davis and his Republican followers below. Democrat Richard Coke had been elected governor in December 1873 over incumbent governor Davis, but Davis contested the election and tried to keep the legislature from convening. Protected by the Love brothers and their comrades, the Fourteenth Legislature organized, and Coke was inaugurated on January 15, 1874. Legend has it that John Love kicked Davis in the butt as he exited through the capitol rotunda door.

Robert Love was sheriff of Limestone County from 1884 to 1890 and United States marshal for the Northern District of Texas from 1894 to 1896. He also served as president of the Sheriffs' Association of Texas from 1886 to 1894. He was elected to the office of state comptroller in 1900.

Love's remains were transported to Tehuacana, where he was buried at the old family home on July 3.

LEGAL LUNACY

It was one o'clock in the afternoon at the Driskill Hotel, April 16, 1908. The opulent lobby was filled with guests when the roar of a shotgun stopped people in their tracks. "The noise was deafening. It sounded like four cannon had gone off at the same time," one witness said.

Austin Bar Association president John Dowell had unloaded the first of four buckshot blasts at San Antonio attorney Mason Williams. Then he drew a revolver, fired one shot and snapped the other cartridges, all of which failed to explode.

Williams was struck by the first two shots, receiving several buckshot in the abdomen. Dowell was a better lawyer than marksman. As soon as Williams saw what Dowell was doing, he pulled his pistol (all the best Texans packed heat back then) and commenced to defend himself, shielding his body behind one of the lobby pillars. He fired several times at Dowell. The first bullet penetrated one of Dowell's legs and then entered the other leg, burying itself in the flesh near an artery.

The downed Dowell was quickly disarmed.

When the shooting began, a number of persons were in the lobby, but in an instant they disappeared, leaving only the two principals and three others. A large crowd swarmed over the scene as soon as the echoes of the shots had died out, and the places where the balls struck the large iron pillars and the stairs were minutely searched out.

After the shooting, Williams turned and walked unaided upstairs to his room, No. 66. Doctors were summoned; Williams smiled and exhibited

Driskill Hotel Lobby. *Courtesy of the Driskill Hotel.*

Driskill Hotel. *Library of Congress Prints and Photographs Division, photograph by Carol M. Highsmith.*

no signs of suffering while Dr. Herman Hill treated his wounds. Three buckshot entered the right side of his abdomen, penetrating possibly half an inch, and five others grazed the flesh. The front of his trousers on the right side was shot into shreds. He took the next train home to San Antonio, where he walked from the sleeping car and was then placed on a stretcher and taken in an ambulance to his home, joking that "my back pains more from riding the distance between here and Austin on this hard couch than do the wounds."

Dowell was carried into a sample room at the Driskill, where Dr. Howard Granberry temporarily dressed his wounds. He was then taken to his home, 503 East Second Street.

The bad feeling started over a trial that had begun in Judge George Calhoun's court the day before, in which Dowell sought to have Williams disbarred from the practice of law. The trial lasted over until the morning of the shooting, when it was postponed until two o'clock because District Attorney Hamilton had been sick and was unable to attend court.

The disbarment proceedings against Williams resulted from bad feelings over recent litigation between Dowell and the West Texas Bank & Trust Company of San Antonio.

Dowell held the Forty-Acre Spring Livestock Company Ranch, a fifteen-thousand-acre tract in Williamson and Travis Counties. The West Texas Bank & Trust Company brought a foreclosure against the ranch, and the court ordered the foreclosure. Williams had represented the bank.

Joe Pattrone was tending bar during the lunch hour, and a group of the state's most prominent attorneys were among the men in his room. Pattrone was not paying much attention to what was said. Judge Charles Ogden, attorney for the fabulous Hetty Green estate, and E.P. Wilmot, president of the Austin National Bank, were talking together. Mason Williams and William Green were also present. Green said that Dowell came in and walked up to him. They exchanged greetings and shook hands.

Dowell then turned to Ogden, who was standing next to Green. A few words passed between them in reference to the litigation in which Dowell and Williams were the principals.

"You have insulted me, Mr. Ogden, and after this litigation is over, you will have to answer for it to me," Dowell said.

Dowell then turned angrily away and went out the barroom's west door. His office was located just back of the Driskill Hotel on Brazos Street. Green said his party remained in the bar a few minutes and then went out into the alley.

Dowell returned minutes later, at the east door. He was in the hotel corridor when Williams walked out of the barroom into the lobby toward the elevator, on his way to lunch in the upstairs dining room.

At that point, he saw Dowell approaching with a double-barreled shotgun. "Of course I knew what he was up to and attempted to dodge behind a large upright column," Williams said, adding that he had known for several weeks that Dowell was liable to take some action and that the affair was not a complete surprise.

Dowell retorted that he was armed that day in the Driskill lobby, not because he intended to shoot Williams, but because he "saw an avenue through the Driskill hotel to avoid any undue publicity during a walk to a pawn brokers shop" where he proposed to pawn the shotgun and pistol to meet a grocery bill. He said that as he walked through the hotel Ogden shot at him and that he was never more surprised in his life. He said that he saw Mason Williams with his gun raised, at which point Dowell fired at Williams.

Several hours after the shooting, complaints were served against Dowell and Williams for assault to murder and against Ogden, Dowell and Williams for carrying pistols.

Some humor came out of the mayhem, mostly involving "furriners" on their first trip to Texas, one of whom had been sitting at the writing desk when the firing began. Instead of running, he quietly sat back and watched the proceedings. As soon as the smoke had cleared, he went to his room, packed his grip and caught the first southbound train out of town.

Dowell's trial for assault to murder took place during the last week of February 1909. His jury consisted of two white farmers, three merchants, one laborer, five businessmen and, a rarity during the days of Jim Crow, a black man. The case was on trial five days. His wife occupied a prominent place in the courtroom throughout the trial.

When Dowell took the stand in his defense on February 25, he became almost hysterical in his testimony and declared that Williams was advancing on him, firing as he did so, and that he fired in self-defense.

Shortly after 6:00 p.m. on February 27, after being out over two hours, the jury returned a verdict of guilty against Dowell for assault with intent to murder Mason Williams. The case had been fought bitterly and contested at every stage. Dowell's punishment was fixed at two years in the penitentiary. He heard the verdict calmly, and his counsel immediately asked for a new trial. Dowell thanked his friends for their support and assured them that the decision would be reversed and the case come out all right in the end. Pending a motion for a new trial, his motion for bond was denied.

COURT-HOUSE AND POST-OFFICE, AUSTIN, TEX.

Courthouse and post office, Austin, Texas. *From* A History of Public Buildings Under the Control of the Treasury Department, *United States Dept. of the Treasury: Hills, Wallace H., comp; Sutherland, John A., comp. Washington, D.C. Government Printing Office. 1901.*

The district court in Austin overruled the motion for a new trial on March 31, whereupon Dowell gave notice of appeal and was freed on $1,000 bail.

On the morning of September 7, Dowell walked into the federal district courtroom with a fully loaded automatic shotgun. The courtroom was swarming with lawyers, many of whom, scenting trouble, made a quick getaway. Judge C.A. Wilcox of the Twenty-sixth District Court was on the bench, calling his docket. Dowell walked across the room and seated himself in the jury box, the gun in his lap. Deputy Sheriff Andy Townsend walked up to Dowell and, taking hold of the gun, said, "You will have to give this to me." Dowell grabbed for the gun, and as they battled for possession, Sheriff George Matthews entered the room and helped disarm Dowell.

Dowell then stood up and addressed the court and remaining members of the bar, declaring in the most vigorous language that he had been maligned, shot, robbed and jailed and that he proposed to get even with all those who had turned against him. He condemned most severely Judge Calhoun of the Fifty-third District Court, not mentioning him by name but threatening to take his life. He had been convicted of assault with intent to murder in Calhoun's court.

Dowell raved so wildly and scattered his threats with such profusion, witnesses claimed, that Matthews locked him up in the county jail and preferred a charge of lunacy against him.

Dowell had made no move with his gun toward anyone, but his threats against Calhoun's life led the officers to believe that Dowell had come to kill him. Calhoun was to have called his court docket at ten o'clock that morning, and Wilcox afterward, but it was decided at the last minute that Wilcox would call his docket first, so Calhoun was not on the bench when Dowell entered the room.

Wilcox had remained silent during Dowell's outburst, but after Dowell had been removed from the courtroom, he said that an offense had been committed against the court's dignity, but considering the mental condition and excitement under which Dowell appeared to be laboring, he would impose no penalty.

A couple days later, Dowell was tried on the charge of lunacy; one hundred witnesses were summoned to testify for and against his insanity. Dowell fought the charge vigorously, contending that he was not insane, just drunk. He admitted that his one great fault was a taste for whisky, which would explain much, if not all, of his explosive behavior over the years.

After a seven-day trial, the jury was dismissed on September 16 because one of the jurymen had discussed the case outside of court. Dowell was arraigned a second time on the same charge.

His new trial commenced on October 7. Dr. Joe Wooten declared that Dowell was suffering from incurable paranoia that appeared spasmodically, and if released, he might kill someone, but the jury sided with Dowell and acquitted him. Dowell had practiced law with Dr. Wooten's brother, Dudley Wooten, in the 1880s.

Dowell may not have been an adjudged lunatic, but he was an undisputable hothead.

Dowell was born in Panola County, Mississippi, in 1850. His father was a surgeon in the Confederate army, and the family moved to Gonzales County after the war. Financed by a well-to-do relative, cattleman and later prominent Austin banker George Littlefield, Dowell completed his education at Washington and Lee University and moved to Austin in 1869. By 1872, he was practicing law and working as a land agent.

Dowell quickly gained a reputation as a skilled, albeit quick-tempered, lawyer. Late in the afternoon of December 8, 1881, during the trial of a man named Gibson for bigamy, he became offended at a remark by county attorney E. Taylor Moore. Dowell, who was defending Gibson, responded by throwing a glass at Moore. Both men were arrested, and Dowell was fined $100.

In February 1885, Dowell and Osceola Archer were engaged in a small civil suit in Justice Thomas Purnell's court. Hot words were passed, and the first thing anybody knew, the two were pummeling each other desperately. Dowell weighed, at best, about half as much as his portly foe but went at Archer with a savage earnestness that showed he meant business. He was met in the same spirit. Judge Purnell called on his constabulary force to interfere. They did so, whereupon hostilities almost immediately ceased. His honor, more in sorrow than in anger, then read the belligerents a sermon that wound up with the remark that they were each indebted five dollars for contempt of court. After the gentlemen shook hands and expressed their sorrow for the foolish fracas, Purnell remitted their fines.

Despite these outbursts (and others not mentioned here), Dowell was elected president of the Austin Bar Association in 1892.

He also served as a senior officer in the state militia during the 1890s, and in February 1893, Governor Stephen Hogg appointed Dowell to the board of managers of the state lunatic asylum at Austin.

Despite his high positions, he continued to live up to his reputation as a hothead. Dowell and Colonel S.O. Cloud were engaged in conversation at the corner of Seventh and Congress Avenue on the morning of March 29, 1894, when James Byrne came up and said, "Mr. Dowell, I want to know why you insulted my niece."

"I never did anything of the kind," Dowell responded.

"You are a goddamned liar," Byrne said, as he hit Dowell over the head with the butt end of a billiard cue.

Dowell fell to the pavement, and as he attempted to rise two or three times, a blow from Byrne sent him down again. Finally, after struggling for about ten feet, Dowell got out his pistol and, while on the ground, fired. The ball struck the pavement and glanced off harmlessly.

Cloud held Byrne by the overcoat collar while he was hitting Dowell, and after the shot was fired, Constable Jim Davis appeared on the scene. He took the pistol from Dowell and helped him get up, whereupon Byrne struck him again before Davis could capture the cue.

Dowell's extensive real estate interests eventually led to his acquisition of the Forty-Acre Spring Ranch. After Dowell lost his case against West Texas Bank & Trust Company to keep the ranch, Sheriff Matthews was given a court order to sell the ranch. At Dowell's lunacy trial, Matthews said that Dowell had accused him and his deputies of theft and other wrongful acts and threatened several times to take Matthews's life and that when he attempted to take Dowell's gun on September 7, Dowell told him he was tired of the way Matthews was treating him.

Williams said he asked Dowell if he had a pistol; Dowell denied it, and when Matthews began searching him, Dowell said, "Goddamn you, can't you take my word for it?" He appeared very excited and proclaimed to the assembled lawyers that he had been robbed by a lot of sons of bitches.

Matthews told of collecting a fine from Dowell a couple years earlier, at which time Dowell told him, "I don't like it a goddamn bit the way you and Monroe Fox are trying to shoot me down like a goddamn dog." But then he said that Dowell had apologized to him on several occasions for his actions.

By 1911, Dowell was practicing law and dealing in real estate in Houston, where he enjoyed a reputation as a skilled attorney and orator, as evidenced by a tribute speech in memory of Richard Maury, criminal district attorney of Harris County who was killed in an automobile accident in April 1914: "The dead eagle lies stretched up on the plain, no more through rolling clouds to soar again. In the passing of Richard G. Maury, the bar, the state and mankind in general have in my judgment sustained a great loss. He gave abundant proof of a long, glorious and useful life. He had all the qualities necessary and time alone awaited their bloom and flower."

Toward the end of 1914, the incurable paranoia that Dr. Wooten had declared Dowell was suffering from, and which appeared spasmodically, seemed to be rearing its ugly head again.

In December 1914, he sued the Houston Ice and Brewing Company, claiming a beer keg fell from a passing truck and struck him in the head, body and legs. He asked for $20,000 in damages. The case was dismissed at his cost in the Fifty-fifth District Court.

In October 1915, Dowell sought damages totaling $3,010 from the City of Houston for two accidents sustained on the streets, due to defective sidewalks. He claimed the sidewalks were uneven, causing him to trip. The accidents occurred in August and September, for each of which he asked $1,505. The claim, in the form of two itemized bills, one for each accident, was presented to the city council bearing a notation from the city solicitor recommending that it be denied. Each carried the same items, the only differences being the location and the injured member. One accident occurred at Main and Capitol, where the right leg was injured, the other at 1108 Liberty Avenue, where the left leg was injured. For the injury proper in each case, he asked

$1,000 for mental anguish and $500 for physical pain. The third item in each bill was for a pair of pants, torn such as to be of no market whatsoever; value $5.

In June 1916, he filed to run for Eighth District congressman. That same month, Harris County sheriff's deputies arrested him on a charge of lunacy, and the county lunacy commission adjudged him of unsound mind on June 15. Several hearings had been held. A large number of witnesses were heard, some of whom said they believed Dowell to be of sound mind.

On July 7, for the second time in two years, Judge William Masterson declared unconstitutional the state lunacy law in the case of Charles Monger, who was released from custody after a hearing in the Fifty-fifth District Court. The statute prescribed a trial before a commission of six physicians. Masterson declared the statute unconstitutional, and his decision was upheld by the higher court. In deference to this decision, the lunacy court sought to try patients by juries. Such patients would not be received by the asylum authorities. In the meantime, more than one inmate of the insane ward at the Harris County jail took advantage of Masterson's decision. John Dowell sued out a writ of habeas corpus, and a hearing was set for the morning of July 8.

Dowell was tried before a jury for lunacy a second time, on the morning of July 14 at the county jail. Holding that his former trial and conviction by a board of physicians were illegal, he acted as his own attorney and beat the case on the second trial.

Dowell was released from custody at the county jail on July 25. He returned to Austin in the company of his son, George, who had promised to take care of him. In the next few months, he fought and won several cases in which others were charged with lunacy.

Dowell died suddenly at his office in the Settegast building in Houston on Friday morning, May 18, 1917. He was seventy-three years old and had been in ill health for a number of years.

As a result of his second lunacy trial, he brought suit for $100,000 damages against Frank Williford of the district attorney's office, who tried the case, and against the jury of physicians who convicted him on the original trial. The suit had not come to trial at the time of his death, having been filed only a few days earlier. A son and daughter came from Austin to retrieve his remains, which were buried in Austin's Oakwood Cemetery.

"TELL BEN I'VE KILLED MOLLIE"

As the sun rose on the morning of Wednesday, April 24, 1912, a pistol shot rang out midway down an alley near the corner of Second and Colorado Streets, in Austin's "tenderloin." Mary W. "Mollie" King, twenty-seven years old, died instantly, shot by her lover, John Henry Brock. The bullet entered the back of her neck near the base of the skull, breaking her neck. The back of her head was badly powder burned.

Brock surrendered to the police shortly afterward.

Jourdon Simmons, the only witness, said that he was chopping kindling in the backyard of Frank Sanford's restaurant at 203 West Second when Brock and King passed him. They had just exited Ben Piper's saloon next door, at the corner of Colorado and Second Streets. They were walking very close together and had just about enough time to walk to the place—he thought about sixty feet—when she fell. Brock came toward him the next minute and ordered Simmons, a black man, to call a doctor.

According to Simmons, Brock said, "Mollie cut me, and I shot her," as he wiped blood from his face. Then he asked Simmons to go and see if she had anything to say or how she was doing. When he returned with the bad news, Brock asked him to call the police instead.

Brock's cut was superficial, a thin downward swipe down one cheek.

Brock went back to Piper's saloon, where they had spent the evening, and told Pat Patterson, the saloon's porter, "Pat, tell Ben I've killed Mollie." Brock and Ben Piper had run another saloon a few years earlier in the "southwest section of the town," as Austin's red-light district was

Deep in the "southwest section of the town." *From the* Social Survey of Austin, *issue 15, of* Bulletin of the University of Texas, *issue 273, William Benjamin Hamilton, University of Texas, 1913. Courtesy E.O. Wilson.*

Palo Pinto County saloon, circa 1906. *Courtesy **Palo Pinto** County Historical Association.*

then known, and Brock had a room upstairs from the saloon at the time of the killing.

"He ordered me to ring up the police," Patterson said. "He asked me to give him a drink, and I refused. Then he walked out and said he was going to the city hall himself."

Night policeman J.C. Wright was second on the scene and found a long knife with blood on its tip about a foot away from King's right hand. Neely Kyzer, a bartender, said that it was Brock's knife.

Brock said only that he was sorry and had acted in self-defense.

Brock and Mollie had met each other eight years earlier at her parents' home in Merrillton in northern Travis County; Brock lived in the adjoining community of McNeil and had worked as a deputy for her father, longtime Travis County constable Lem King. Sometime in 1906, she left home under cloudy circumstances and came to Austin to live. Brock paid some of her medical bills, moving expenses and her board until he came to Austin soon afterward, having, it was said at his trial, abandoned his family at McNeil. Brock went into the saloon business, and the pair took up residence in a room over his "Blazing Stump" resort in old Guy Town, where she often tended bar and served drinks to "women of the lowest type."

They lived together for four years, he said, before his wife "came up square with us."

"I told my wife I loved Mollie King better than her and if she could not stand it she could quit me; but I promised to raise and educate my children."

And make more babies. Despite his affair with King, he did not entirely abandon his wife. She and the kids moved to Austin, and the couple had four children here beginning in 1907, the last being born on August 27, 1911.

It appears that all was not well between the lovebirds in the days before Mollie's death. Several people testified that on the day and evening before the killing, Brock had been quite agitated about their relationship.

Naomi Luck, a well-known lady about the tenderloin district, met Brock less than an hour before the killing at Piper's, where she had gone to get a drink of whiskey. As she approached the window, she saw Brock sitting just inside. He was busy with a knife, whittling or paring his nails. He had been out in the Texas Panhandle on a business trip. Well acquainted with King and Brock, Luck struck up a conversation, asking Brock when he had gotten back into town.

"Last night."

"How is the old hen—Mollie?"

"Oh, we're squabbling all the time. I guess I'll have to kill the damned old whore to get rid of her."

The bartender brought her whiskey and passed it out through the window to her; she paid her dime and went on her way. "You can hear such stuff every day down there," she said, "and I didn't pay any attention to his threat."

Arriving at the death scene about five minutes after the shot rang out, she noticed what appeared to be the same knife on the ground near Mollie's body.

Neely Kyzer, bartender at Piper's saloon, said that at Brock's request, he had taken a bottle of whiskey to him in his room over Piper's saloon Tuesday afternoon, at which time Brock asked him about King, "implying that he thought her affections might be alienated from him." Kyzer said he told Brock that if Mollie was disloyal, he didn't know about it. Neely's brother, Arthur, had been killed in Brock's saloon the year before.

Mrs. Mattie Kyzer, mother of Neely and Arthur, who kept the boardinghouse at 307 West Fifth where Mollie King was staying, said she had seen Mollie early in the evening Tuesday but that later one of the boarders told her that King had "gone to the depot," presumably the MKT "Katy" train depot at Third and Congress.

That evening, Brock came to the back door of the Kyzer house and asked to come in. There was some debate among the residents, who all knew him, as to whether or not they should let Brock in. Lee Whatley, a local coffee roaster, decided to admit him, and as he opened the door, he saw Brock had his hand on his gun. On being told that Mollie was not home, he asked how long she had been gone and when she would return. He asked to be shown to her room. Upon entering her room, he still had his hand on his gun. After looking around, he lit a match and—again, hand on gun—looked under the bed. Finding nothing, he left.

Edgar East, who worked for the street railway company, said that he ran into Brock in a tenderloin saloon that night and heard him say, "I'll kill the goddamned whore before the sun rises."

On the afternoon of the killing, Mrs. Brock and two of their children visited Brock in jail, and two of their sons took him his supper. Other visitors during his first day of incarceration were brother Coon Brock and Pastor W.D. Bradfield. Brock "talked with reserve," according to reports.

John Henry Brock was born on January 20, 1868, in Winnfield, Louisiana. He married Mary Josephine Williams in 1888, in Merle, Burleson County.

They moved back to Winnfield for several years before returning to Texas in 1894, settling in northern Travis County, where he was a foreman at Austin White Lime & Cement Company at McNeil for several years before becoming a Travis County deputy constable. In 1904, he and Mollie's father went to arrest two men living near Cele, about twenty-eight miles northeast of Austin, on a charge of aggravated assault. The pair had barricaded themselves in the house and swore they would never surrender, whereupon Brock kicked in the door. As he entered, he was met with a point-blank shotgun blast that passed between his legs and tore away his coattail. The wanted men were arrested and lodged in the Travis County Jail.

Constable King was a "bulldozer" with a reputation for always getting his man. There were men who thought they were tough and would "bluff" Lem King, but they inevitably wound up in the Travis County hoosegow with bruised heads. King used the butt of his pistol on their heads, and his reputation for subduing unruly men became so well known that anyone he had an arrest warrant for either came in peacefully or skipped the country.

There is often a thin line between lawbreaker and law enforcer, and Brock crossed the line more than once. He got into a row with Tom Scantlain in September 1905 at McNeil and cut him up rather badly with a knife. He was tried for assault to murder, found guilty and fined.

At 10:30 a.m. on June 1, 1911, Joe Ash, who kept a restaurant in the rear of Brock's saloon at 206 West Fourth, was shot dead; Arthur Kyzer, employee of the city's street department, lay mortally wounded. The tragedy followed a quarrel over a baseball bet on the San Antonio Bronchos–Austin Senators series of games. Who shot Kyzer was a mystery. As he lay dying in the city hospital, Kyzer only said it wasn't Ash. He and all the witnesses said it was a third person. Kyzer died the day after the shooting.

Police arrested Brock, Arch Houston, Ab Boutwell, Carrie Broley and George Kerns, hoping that at least one of them would reveal the name of Kyzer's killer.

Kyzer's autopsy revealed that he had been hit twice—once with a lead bullet and again with a steel jacket .38-caliber—leading the police to conclude that two people were involved in his killing.

As a result, President Allen of the Texas Baseball League announced he would employ detectives to assist in stopping baseball game betting and asked county attorneys all over the state to assist in prosecuting cases.

The murders were never solved.

Brock's trial for the murder of Mollie King commenced four weeks after her death. Throughout the first day, the courtroom was crowded to suffocation. Brock was entirely at ease. His brother sat beside him, and his little boy, Bill, embraced him for a moment that afternoon. Brock smoked a cigar during recesses and went at will around the room.

"Did you intend to kill Mollie King?" the prosecuting attorney asked Brock after he took the stand in his defense. The hundreds of men in the crowded courtroom leaned forward expectantly to hear his plea.

"God knows I did not. It was an accident. I considered her the best friend, the only true friend I had in the world. I certainly had no purpose, no motive for slaying Mollie, the woman I loved more than everyone else on the earth."

There was a collective gasp of mingled surprise and disbelief at the word "accident." Everyone expected Brock to plead self-defense.

Brock said that Mollie had sent him money for his trip from the Panhandle (a money order receipt showing she had sent him five dollars at Fort Worth a few days earlier was found in her purse at the coroner's inquest) and that they had spent Tuesday afternoon and night at Piper's before slipping out about five o'clock in the morning, "so's not to wake Ben Piper."

"We went out, arm in arm, talking pleasantly and the best friends in the world. She called me 'Daddy' when in a playful mood. 'Daddy,' she said, 'you got any change? I have some little bills to pay.' I told her I had a little silver in my pocket, and she reached in to get the change."

When he had gotten home from the Panhandle a few days earlier, she met him at the station, and they shook hands, he said. "We were friends then, but it wouldn't have done for us to be seen on the streets together—a woman of her business—so she went on one street and I another."

He said he was drunk when he got to Austin and was never fully sober until he got in jail and that they were together every night until her death, for at least a few hours, knocking drinks back, but only at night, because he couldn't be with her "in daytime." Strange words from the man who had been instrumental in her fall from grace.

She was commonly considered to be a "lady of the night," but city directories indicate that she did not live in houses of prostitution—Mrs. Kyzer ran a respectable boardinghouse and worked at Bosche's Troy Laundry—and that Mollie held down legitimate jobs as milliner and "head trimmer" at Scarbrough's Department Store.

There were those who claimed that she had expressed a wish to quit her old life and "live right." Even Brock admitted that she had gone into a legitimate business.

But, he claimed on the witness stand, she was the jealous half of their relationship. He admitted the knife was his—that another woman, Lee Talbot, had given it to him. When Mollie reached in his pocket for the change, she found the knife, grabbed it and flew into a passion. She swore that he must take the knife back to Lee, and he agreed to do so.

Then he told of other times when she would fly into a jealous fury and threaten to kill him. "She never wanted me to visit another woman, though she didn't object when I spent the night with my family."

She took the knife that morning, he claimed, cursing him because he had lied to her. He caught her hand with the knife in it, and the struggle began. She cut him and then, he said, "while I still had her hand, the scuffle threw her back against my stomach. I had my pistol. It is easy on trigger. I punched her in the neck with the pistol, thinking to stun her. The second time I punched her, the revolver went off. I held her in my arms until I saw she was dead or seriously hurt. Then I dropped her and sent for the doctor, greatly excited and thinking only of her.

Scarbrough & Sons—Austin's big department store. *From* Austin Yesterday and Today: A Glance at Her History, a Word About Her Enterprises, a Description of Her Big Banking Establishment, *Jackson, Pearl Cashell. Austin, TX: Press of E.L. Steck, 1915.*

"If I ever made any threats to kill Mollie, I was either drunk or crazy, and certainly did not mean it."

The jury took an hour to reach a verdict of guilty, exactly one month after the tragedy.

He didn't wince, didn't turn pale. He carried the same bearing of bravado that had characterized him throughout the trial, even smiling on occasion.

Mollie's mother, on the other hand, strode in front of Brock, with a sort of happiness depicted on her face, and Brock's face clouded for a moment. Then she began laughing and crying all in one.

Governor Oscar Colquitt. *Library of Congress Prints and Photographs Division.*

He was sentenced to hang on December 21 but was saved with only hours to spare by his attorneys, who presented affidavits from his mother and wife to Judge Calhoun that put his sanity into doubt. He was tried on the grounds of insanity and adjudged sane.

He was scheduled to die on March 21, but on March 18, Governor Oscar Colquitt granted a respite until May 23 to allow him and the Board of Pardons to consider commuting Brock's sentence to life imprisonment, a move surprisingly supported by a number of social conservatives, including the Reverend "Fighting Bob" Shuler, who led the fights to shut down Austin's red-light district in 1913 and for prohibition in 1918.

They blamed the ills of society for the Mollie King tragedy.

Brock was baptized into the East Avenue Baptist Church in a prison bathtub on May 23 by childhood playmate J.L. Watson. His mother, wife and all nine children had just called on the governor to beg for mercy.

On May 29, Governor Colquitt passed on the Board of Pardons' recommendation to let the law take its course.

Brock, dressed in a black suit, walked silently from the death cell at 3:22 p.m. on May 30, 1913, to the second-story gallows with Sheriff Matthews and Deputy S. Schmidt on either side.

A huge crowd had gathered around the county courthouse and jail upon news that Brock would hang at 1:00 p.m. They crowded into the courthouse corridors, adjoining streets and alley, and some tried to see through the barred window into the death chamber. A number of police officers helped the sheriff's department handle the two-hundred-odd curiosity seekers crammed into the jail.

Save for a few words by Reverend J.L. Watson, a prayer by Reverend W.D. Bradfield and three maidens who sang "Shall We Gather at

"The hour has come." *From* On a Mexican Mustang Through Texas: From the Gulf to the Rio Grande, *by Sweet and Knox, Chatto and Windus, Piccadilly, 1884.*

the River," not a word was said. Brock appeared oblivious to the gallows proceedings.

After he slept fairly well and ate a hearty last breakfast, his wife, mother, nine children, brothers and other relatives crowded into the death cell that morning to say goodbye. Brock broke down and wept but quickly recovered and gave them words of comfort. Sheriff Matthews allowed them as much time as they wanted, but they left after about thirty minutes.

His last words were written on five sheets of paper. He blamed the state for all that had happened to him, that the state permitted the evil conditions to exist that caused his downfall, that the state furnished the cup and placed it to his lips, the contents of which poisoned his soul and brain, and while in this condition he accidentally killed a human being. He was paying for a

Cell, Gonzales County Jail, 1887. *Photo by Samantha Zelade.*

crime that he had not committed but for indiscretion in "pushing that woman with my pistol."

He stood on the trapdoor and folded his hands behind him so that the officers could bind them together. He remained erect and showed no signs of weakness as the black cap was placed over his head. The noose was adjusted, and Sheriff Matthews sprung the trap at 3:31 p.m. Brock was pronounced dead three minutes and thirty-two seconds later.

John Henry Brock had the distinction of being the last man to drop from the Travis County Jail gallows. He is buried in Austin's Oakwood Cemetery.

Gallows, Gonzales County Jail, 1887. *Photo by Samantha Zelade.*

But there's more to be told. Willie Kemp and his family lived in the Merrillton neighborhood when Willie was a youngster, moving away about the time Mollie and Brock moved to Austin. Kemp knew both families, and in his memoir, *True Tales of Central Texas*, he tells "the rest of the story."

When Mollie and younger sister Estella were in their teens, they—like so many of their peers—grew weary of being farm girls and decided to explore the larger world on their own. On their way, they met Brock, who induced them to taste liquor. As was so often the case, they liked the giddy, tingle-all-over feeling it brought. One drink led to another until Mollie lost her self-control. Brock being a rather good-looking and smooth-talking man, she gave her all to him while Estella recovered her senses and went home.

Given what we know, it is reasonable to assume that Brock got Mollie pregnant and paid for an abortion since no child was born.

It is here that the story turns even more sinister. Estella, like Mollie, was "healthy, pretty, sweet, full of life and with a burning desire to live life to the fullest."

After Mollie eloped with Brock, Estella appeared to settle down and behave, telling her mama that she was "traveling the straight and narrow path." Mama King, in her "agony, disgrace, shame and distress over losing one daughter to a life of shame and disgrace, became alarmed at the prospect of losing another the same way." Mrs. King kept a close watch on Estella and did not like what she saw, to the extent that she was heard to have declared, "Desperate diseases require desperate remedies." And so, according to Kemp, Estella—barely twenty—died a "sudden and violent death, while in apparently good health" in December 1906, leading neighbors to believe that Mrs. King had poisoned her so as to prevent any possibility of her following in Mollie's footsteps. There was no autopsy.

On the eve of her death, according to Kemp, Mollie told Brock that she "was going home to Mama." She had tired of her life with Brock and asked her parents' forgiveness, which they accepted. She went home all right, but in a casket. Her parents buried her in the Merrillton cemetery.

Folks in the community wondered why a bulldozer like Lem King did not come to a showdown with Brock; it was customary at the time that when a man mistreated another man's women folk, the offended party took the offender to task, to the point of shooting him on sight. King had proven as constable that he had no problems killing a man.

But then, life is full of mystery. And the Kings did have the ultimate pleasure of watching Henry Brock drop.

ADAMANT JOHNSON

Austin city health officer Dr. C.W. Goddard walked into city manager Adam Johnson's office at city hall shortly before 11:00 a.m. on Monday, March 26, 1927.

Goddard appeared smilingly at his office, Johnson said, and presented a paper concerning a contract for sewer work. Johnson, seated at his desk, told Goddard it was a water department matter.

Without a word of warning, Goddard drew an automatic pistol and began firing. City engineer O.E. Metcalf came in from an adjoining room when he heard the shots, seized Goddard and held him until police chief J.N. Littlepage arrived and placed Goddard in the city jail. Metcalf said Goddard was calm and made no resistance.

Johnson, Austin's first city manager, was taken to Seton infirmary with five pistol shot wounds.

Goddard was found dead in the city jail at 2:30 p.m. He had slashed his throat and cut one of his wrists with a penknife that officers had overlooked. He had made no statement concerning his attack on Johnson.

Chief Littlepage found Goddard's body. He had been dead at least an hour. Goddard, sixty, was survived by his wife and several grown children. His body was returned to his home in Bell County for burial.

Johnson was reported late Monday as steadily improving, and attending physicians said his chances for recovery were good. Five shots struck Johnson: two in the left breast and two in the back, with a fifth wound on a finger. Johnson's body wounds were serious but not dangerous.

None of the bullets penetrated the abdominal cavity. Johnson never lost consciousness.

Dr. Goddard had served as state health officer during Governor William P. Hobby's administration, coming to Austin from Holland in Bell County, where he had practiced medicine for many years. He later was appointed health officer of the University of Texas, serving in that capacity until 1926, when he was appointed head of Austin's health department. If Johnson showed any remorse over Goddard's death, it was in private.

The two had been on the outs for several weeks; Johnson had been criticizing Dr. Goddard's work. It was said that Goddard accused Johnson of having made a recommendation to the city council for his dismissal. It was Johnson's style.

Johnson was born in Burnet in 1872, son of ex-Confederate general Adam Rankin Johnson, the blind man who founded the town of Marble Falls. After serving in the Spanish-American War, Johnson came back to Burnet and established a mercantile business in 1905. He was appointed to the Burnet County Draft Board during World War I but resigned to serve his country once more. He sold his business, moved his family to Austin and went to officer training school, attaining the rank of major. After the war, he moved to Wichita Falls, which was experiencing an oil boom, and got into the real estate business. In 1920, Governor Hobby appointed him to the State Board of Control, where he served until October 1921, when he resigned to run the Adam Johnson Company on Congress Avenue.

In 1923, he became president of the Austin Chamber of Commerce, with the objective of establishing the city manager form of government in Austin. In 1924, the council-manager initiative won an election with a scant forty-two-vote margin. The election was contested and hung in the courts through 1925. In the meantime, Johnson went to Corpus Christi to work in construction.

The city manager faction won the court battle in 1926.

On Saturday night, June 29, newly elected councilman and business partner Dave Reed asked Johnson to serve thirty days as city manager until the permanent appointee could take over. He was sworn into office, along with the newly elected city council, on July 1. Three days later, he had abolished four city positions and begun a career that would last seven turbulent years.

Johnson knew the job would be tough, and he tackled it like the no-nonsense businessman he was—bluntly and without diplomacy—instead of like a savvy politician, which would have made his life and job a lot easier, especially when it came to the Goddard affair.

Soon after taking office, the *Austin American-Statesman* carried a photo of Johnson standing in a hole, knee-deep in water from a leak costing the city fifty thousand gallons a day. The city itself was in a hole, drowning in delinquent taxes, surviving on light and water revenues.

He began nine hundred suits for delinquent taxes, sometimes against close friends. But by 1927, the city was operating on a cash basis. He spearheaded moves that, while cherished as part of the Austin lifestyle today, weren't popular in all quarters then, such as building the Barton Springs swimming pool we enjoy today.

The gun was in Johnson's hand on October 9, 1928, when Armando Alexander, a black man, shot and killed Marshal Littlepage, two black women and a white carpenter. Alexander shot Katherine Pyburn, forty-five, and her daughter, Ethel, twenty-four. Littlepage went after him and was shot three times with a shotgun, dying shortly afterward in a hospital. In his flight, Alexander shot Joe Blunt, who had been working on a house nearby, in the chin.

Upon learning of Littlepage's death, Johnson gave orders to city officers to shoot to kill. He then went home after his own deer rifle to join in the chase. Police were about to close in on Alexander when he managed to turn the long shotgun against himself and pull the trigger.

No one knew why he shot the two black women and Blunt. Alexander was believed to have been "temporarily deranged."

Alexander was twenty-seven years old. His wife said he started on a rampage after attempting to take her out on a narrow road, threatening to kill her. She jumped from the automobile and escaped him.

Littlepage had joined the Austin police department as a detective about 1914. He became chief of police on May 1, 1924. He had been in the grocery business prior to his police service here.

Several times during the summer of 1929, marauding army air corps student fliers from San Antonio's Kelly Field attacked downtown Austin.

In one raid, a solo flier nosedived Lake Austin Boulevard, tearing down a rooftop radio aerial and an electric power line and then stripping a chinaberry tree of its leaves before winging his way home.

The day before, three other daredevils had skimmed downtown rooftops, "scaring people half to death," Johnson told the *American-Statesman*. "With a roar that sounded like a tornado, the big planes dipped low as they went toward the airport, and a lot of persons flinched, thinking that the roof was about to cave in on them, or that a fire truck was loose." Next, they buzzed Johnson's north Austin house. "I thought they were going to run over me," he told reporters.

Was it karma or payback from one of many citizens Johnson had alienated?

Johnson promptly telephoned the police and told them to arrest and fine the errant fliers. But when the responsibility could not be placed on anyone, the fliers were allowed to return to San Antonio with the promise that the incident would be reported to their commanding officers.

Being the man he was, Johnson did nothing to burnish his tarnished reputation, and in the 1933 city council race, the unpopular Johnson was the central issue. The anti-Johnson faction won.

When the new city council elected Tom Miller mayor (mayors were not directly elected in those days), Johnson announced that he would not be a candidate for reappointment, and the Miller council's first act was to fire Johnson, who—as the city charter specified—had the authority to make day-to-day decisions at city hall. Miller ignored the charter and ruled Austin his way for twenty-two years, becoming a legend in Texas politics.

Johnson went to work for the National Municipal Association briefly before being asked to head the Texas Relief and Rehabilitation Commission, which, like before, he ruled with an iron fist. While director, he recommended that men on the relief rolls who spent the money given them on liquor instead of food and clothing for their families be thrown into a bull pen and handed a sledge hammer to work out their fines breaking rocks at fifty cents a day and short rations.

He was fired but fought back in court and was restored to office, whereupon the legislature abolished the commission and created a new department of public welfare, which Johnson ran in his typical heavy-handed manner until running afoul of the politicians yet again. With the advent of World War II, he returned to draft board service, in Travis County, serving until 1943, when he retired from public life.

Johnson died after a long illness on February 12, 1952, in Seton Hospital.

BIBLIOGRAPHY

NEWSPAPERS

Austin American-Statesman
Austin City Gazette
Austin Daily Statesman
Austin Sentinel
Flake's Bulletin (Galveston)
Galveston Daily News
Rolling Stone (Austin)
San Antonio Light
San Antonio News
Southern Intelligencer
Texas Siftings (Austin)
Tri-Weekly Gazette (Austin)

BOOKS

Bowen, William A. *Chained Lightning, a Book of Fun*. New York: J.S. Ogilvy & Company, 1883.
Kemp, Willie. *True Tales of Central Texas, as Told by Willie Kemp*. Austin, TX: Willie Kemp, 1979.

Bibliography

Saylor, Steven. *A Twist at the End: A Novel of O. Henry & the Austin, Texas Servant Girl Murders of 1885*. New York: Simon & Schuster, 2000.

Sweet, Alexander, and J. Armoy Knox. *On a Mexican Mustang Through Texas, From the Gulf to the Rio Grande*. Hartford, CT: S.S. Scranton & Co., 1883.

————. *Sketches from* Texas Siftings. New York: Texas Siftings Publishing Co., 1882.

————. *Three Good Stories from* Texas Siftings. New York: J.S. Ogilvy & Company, 1887.

Walton, William. *Life and Adventures of Ben Thompson, Famous Texan*. Austin, TX: W.M. Walton, 1884.

Zelade, Richard. *Guy Town by Gaslight*. Charleston, SC: The History Press, 2014.

Other Sources

Handbook of Texas Online
Wikipedia

ABOUT THE AUTHOR

Richard Zelade is a collector and teller of Texas tales: heroes, outlaws, fussin' and feuds, real tales, tall tales, small tales, music, whores, wars, sex, drugs, roll and rock, eccentricities, legends, characters, roadside attractions, tasty grub.

Richard Zelade was born in Brazoria County, Texas. He received a BA from the University of Texas at Austin in 1975, with honors and special honors in history.

Zelade began writing professionally in 1976. His work has appeared in *Texas Parks & Wildlife*, *Texas Monthly*, *Texas Highways*, *People*, *Southern Living*, *American Way* and many other publications. He is the author of several regional Texas guidebooks and several more books about the scandalous side of Austin history.

A multidisciplinary historian, Zelade studies Texas geology, weather, geography, flora, fauna and ethnic folkways, including the medicinal and food uses of native plants.

ALSO BY RICHARD ZELADE

Austin. Gulf Publishing, 1985.
Austin in the Jazz Age. The History Press, 2015.
Guy Town by Gaslight: A History of Vice in Austin's First Ward. The History Press, 2014.
Hill Country. Gulf Publishing, 1984.
Riding Through Central Texas: 22 Cycle Excursions. Violet Crown Press, 1981.

CONTRIBUTOR TO/CO-AUTHOR OF

The Book of Texas Days, by Ron Stone. Shearer Publishing, 1985.
Como La Flor, a biography of Selena by Joe Nick Patoski. Little-Brown, 1996.
Tastes & Tales from Texas, a cookbook by Peg Hein. Hein & Associates, 1984.
Tastes & Tales from Texas, Volume II, by Peg Hein. Hein & Associates, 1987.
Texas: The Texas Monthly Guidebook, 2nd ed. Texas Monthly Press, 1988. Author of Austin and Dallas chapters.
Texas: The Texas Monthly Guidebook, 3rd ed. Gulf Publishing, 1992. Author of Austin and Hill Country chapters.